THE HUMAN BEHAVIOR

Valentin Matcas, M.Ed.

DEDICATION

I dedicate this book to everyone eager to learn and develop
continuously throughout life.

CONTENTS

1 YOUR TRUE BEHAVIOR

Your behavior consists of everything that you do in life, knowingly and unknowingly. Even more, your behavior represents and is a consequence of everything that you need, mean, and think throughout life. Yet it was so easy to manage your life if your behavior was so easy to define, because you always live your life alongside the rest of society, and always influenced by the rest of the world, in every manner. You are a social value, highly useful to others, and this is how others end up controlling you and your behavior according to their own needs and reasoning, with or without your consent. And this is how you behave and live your life in society, you influence and you are influenced by others continuously, according to your needs, beliefs, duties, capabilities, orders, and agendas. And you do so successively, continuously, and many times simultaneously throughout life and throughout society.

Even more, your social behavior does not define you entirely, since your private, hidden behavior is distinct from your open, social one. You work hard to keep this shadow behavior unnoticed and at bay, but now when you consider it, you realize that it defines you more than everything else. This has always been the case, it can make life fun and exciting at times, yet it can become dangerous and expensive. Because it has become a continuously hidden need that you are forced to fulfill consistently, and many times, you would rather avoid this private behavior, if you only knew how.

What happens is that the entire world lives in this major dissociation, because everybody seeks privacy and intimacy in life for various reasons, as everybody lives in the hiding most of the time, overwhelmed, guilty, and confused. And now, you seek to find out why you behave in this manner, you want to know what you can do in order to change and improve your behavior, you seek to know how to educate your children towards adopting a good behavior in life and in the world, and this is why you read this book.

Throughout this book, you learn everything about the human behavior, everything necessary to help you control yourself, understand others, and develop to higher levels, along with everything necessary for you to help and educate others to behave well, while developing consistently to higher levels.

Behaviors are more than conscious, unconscious, accepted, hidden, or forbidden. This is why you can never control your behavior by following only what they teach you in school, by following laws and social norms diligently throughout life, by watching and learning from TV, by following various ideologies, or by monitoring and studying your own actions, desires, and tendencies throughout life. You strive to control your behavior in this manner but you fail, and whatever you do, it never seems enough. Because your vices persist, while your lifelong development and your lifelong achievements tend to remain below expectations.

What can you do? You must seek accurate knowledge about the human behavior, to use it in order to develop to the point where you are capable to define and master your own behavior. It is this simple. The problem is that you cannot find accurate knowledge about anything related to genuinely developed humans, but you find only invalid, dogmatic, and even harmful knowledge. And this is done on purpose, through invalid science, through social stereotypes, and through direct censorship.

For example, when you study closely all movies, you find all characters drinking alcohol every time they meet friends, every time they are alone, every time they study, every time they are entertained, and every time life becomes more tedious. And they end up drinking every minute or so in the movie, even unnecessarily, beyond the human capacity, while they still act normally and fit with each glass they drink and with each cigarette they smoke, significantly improved. Your stereotype now consists in having a drink continuously, this is what you do, this is what your family learns to do, your mind is harmed irreparably, and then life really becomes out of control, both in your family and in society, soon to become unbearable. Since this is the trap you fall in.

While this is the case with all addictions, as your anger is trained by all movies, along with your love, harassment, compassion, greed, selfishness, betrayal, social competition, carelessness, and hate. Yet in order to learn more about the human behavior, you must study all common feelings and attitudes. Because some may have roots in the intelligent human behavior, while others may be implemented in your behavior on purpose, consensually, for various reasons. You have to be able to distinguish what is good from what is bad, and what is natural from what is consensual. You have to be able to control and conduct your own reasoning in this manner, since through your reasoning, you may achieve to control your own behavior. Yet what you do, despite your failures, you still follow your row models, you follow their instincts and stereotypes, still striving to adjust your behavior accordingly, and through it, still hoping to be able to integrate in your family and in society, as best as you can. And so life goes on, one day after another, and one social problem at a time. And so you get in trouble through your own bad behavior, repeatedly. Society blames you, and so you endure continuously, while blaming and hating yourself.

This happens throughout this world, and not only with you. While now, it seems suspicious. Because everybody is human, while everybody gets in trouble through their bad behavior, which may be natural and stereotypical.

Could this common, worldwide behavior be in fact the normal, natural human behavior, since everybody is human? Then why should humans have to get in trouble through their own natural human behavior, mostly when they are born in this manner? Are humans really born criminals and sinners by default? Or there is someone somewhere, trying to change and control something, by altering the human behavior, and through it, by altering and controlling humanity itself? Because if this is the case, then it has been going on for some time now, and it is about time that it is studied closely and understood.

Or you do not have to reason at all throughout life, since you may follow only your attitudes, beliefs, and stereotypes directly, and it works. You may follow all orders unconditionally, coming from your authorities and supervisors, and in this manner, you are doomed to live your life continuously through a consensually induced behavior, within a consensually created environment, from one implemented problem to another. Because whenever you have life figured out stereotypically, then this world always takes you by surprise. Because the laws and rules change on you, as all fashions do, what was common now becomes old, ignored, unaccepted, and forbidden, and you are back where you started, having to figure it out all over again, from one problem to the next. Because it may not be you to blame after all, but the social environment, with its laws, regulations, row models, standards, and expectations, along with the rest of your consensual environment, since these are always contradicting themselves while they are the ones deciding your entire social behavior, and through it, your entire life.

Because laws and rules always seem to regulate behaviors. And in order to be able to cope with justice and society, you always end up regulating and censoring yourself, continuously. While you do so against your will, against your own natural needs, and through your own agreement.

This is called consensual behavior. It is consensual and not natural, it goes against your will and human nature, and it can certainly harm you while interfering with your normal, natural meaning and fulfillment. And as you notice, your consensual behavior is part of an entire consensual human society, part of an entire consensual human civilization, which is part of an entire Consensual Matrix, which spans most of the wider world, engulfing humanity altogether.

Why exactly should humans have to live life in sufferance, guilt, and concealment, within this human society, by these human laws, while nothing makes sense? What really happens is that you may, could, and should have been able to live an intelligent human life, on higher developmental levels, under a variety of intelligent human modes of life, switched naturally through your intelligent human cognition, in order to match your higher level intelligent human environment. Or this is the case if you only knew how, if you only could, and if you were only allowed. But you are not, through consensual constraints. Therefore, now you behave consensually, rigidly, disconnected, as in a predefined consensual matrix, as society requires.

Because you have to engage your own reasoning throughout life in order to question yourself and this world for what you do in this world and for what this world does to you. Because behaviors are very complex in nature, and therefore very tedious to understand and conduct, since they have a multitude of characteristics and they come in various distinct modes and levels. And you should know everything before attempting to adjust your own behavior in any manner, or before attempting to educate others and change their behavior. If not, then every time you attempt to change and control yourself stereotypically and unknowingly, you end up reconstructing, following, and enforcing this same consensual, harmful behavior, on you and on those around. And so you are doomed to perpetuate this entire harmful, consensual, nonhuman social environment, endlessly.

For example, at the second developmental level, which is the animal level, you control your second level behavior mostly subconsciously, and you do so by following specific laws and row models that you find in society, media, and entertainment.

While at this second animal intuitive level, you do what it always works for you, thinking directly through needs, attitudes, and stereotypes, while you follow your instincts and feelings continuously. And so you conduct your second level behavior and second level life, regardless of consequences. While you do what others do, and it still works for them, and for you.

This is good and bad. It is good because it allows you to subsist within a society where everyone does just the same, while it is bad because common, stereotypical behaviors are not necessarily favorable for you, for your family, and for the entire society. As it is the case with the use of all legal drugs.

Many behavioral row models implemented through media, science, and education are ideological in nature, and therefore they are consensual, carefully constructed, contradicting sometimes your natural needs and tendencies. Simultaneously, just because some or many of your needs, attitudes, and tendencies remain natural, this does not mean that they are bad, savage, selfish, or evil. Therefore, what society wants from you does not work, or at least it does not work on a longer term. And this forces you to adopt an entire new second life, where you get to fulfill your unaccepted natural needs, a life that you have to disconnect, hide, and live in private, or only with your family and close friends, for as long as you are allowed.

Natural, untamed behaviors may be good, bad, favorable, or unfavorable, and they can get you in trouble, many times badly. Yet by questioning them, along with questioning the laws forbidding them, you are on your way toward a rigorous reasoning behavior, toward finding an equilibrium in life, between the social life and the private life. If you succeed to find out why parts of your natural behavior are forbidden in society today, how and on whose behalf, you are getting closer to your aspiring third level behavior, which is the intelligent human behavior. We study closely all types of behavior, behavioral characteristics, and behavioral levels throughout this book.

If you want to learn more about the human behavior, you must study your own natural, unaltered behavior first, and you must be able to distinguish it from the consensual, standardized behavior demanded continuously from you by society, through laws, norms, fashions, tendencies, social competition, and social regulation.

The human behavior is very complex, and therefore it can become tedious to model and understand. Currently, this study is done by psychology, sociology, and education, mostly through two major old structures: behaviorism and cognitivism. These are ideologies in themselves, since they are empiric in nature, based on statistics and beliefs. And even when considered together, behaviorism and cognitivism lack the necessary knowledge and complexity to explain the human behavior well enough to allow you the capability to control, manage, and adjust your own behavior. And this explains the primitive social state of this world today, with rulers and politicians stealing from the common good of their nations, while together entraining the people to harm themselves and this world methodically.

Because if the current science could model and explain the human cognition and the human behavior, then humanity could control these continuously, in an intelligent manner, and we had a better world, at the intelligent human level. Which is not the case.

As a whole, the current human knowledge in general remains insufficient to allow humans to maintain and control their behavior at the intelligent human level. Therefore, people have to behave and live their lives on lower behavioral levels, sick and disabled, many times addicted to anything, or in servitude, making possible all these tyrants throughout the upper social levels. Or they have to live life through animal instincts, while not being able to control their behavior entirely even at these very low developmental levels. Parents and teachers remain incapable to reach and educate everybody accordingly, and children fail to reach their intelligent human developmental level in early childhood when they should. And this is enough now to explain all the problems in this world, since these have their causes in society, and in its very low developmental level. And this is the case just because science and education are based on ideologies and not on accurate knowledge, and therefore what they teach and apply in this world is not rigorous knowledge, but dogma. Because ideologies are always dogmatic in nature regardless if they are social, religious, or scientific, since they are simple sets of beliefs and not tangible, pertinent, genuine accurate facts.

Do you want to understand and control yourself and your behavior? You need accurate facts in order to learn how to control yourself, and not statistics, dogma, theories, assumptions, and beliefs. How can you learn more about the human behavior in order for you to be able to control yourself, in order for you to be able to teach your children and students to behave well, and in order for you to be able to understand those around along with the entire society? Yet you have to find a way to go beyond science with its cognitivism and behaviorism. You have to break apart all knowledge that these implement, and to find a way to discern what is accurate, true, genuine, and favorable from everything that they claim. Which is not an easy task, because you need new, accurate disciplines to use in order to overcome and replace the current ones, and there are none. Or you may skip all scientific ideologies altogether, by starting your own comprehensive research from scratch, using only genuine, accurate facts, and doing so in a rigorous, analytical, rational manner. And this is what this entire book series does.

What exactly do you do in life? What is there significant enough in your life to grasp your entire time and effort and to define now your entire behavior? You probably seek a good career and education and this keeps you occupied for now, as it is the case with everyone else. But you also sleep naked, and you even walk naked around your bedroom, and you love it. You party on weekends in every manner as everyone else, you drink and smoke all things and you interact with your neighbors and friends even intimately, while you are too old, you are already married, or if not, then you are too young and still in school. Do you sell favors too? Do you troll and bully around while feeling thrilled about it? Are you insolent on purpose with those around including your loved ones, while you never care? Do you go through incredible diets in ways that only you know about? Do you cheat and steal, whenever no one notices?

You might do some or all the above, along with much more, yet your problem could be not this private behavior in itself, and not even the guilt and the illegality that it brings. Besides, some of the examples above are not actually bad behavior, but they are only considered by society to be bad, terrible, and forbidden, many times on purpose, for many reasons.

There is more taking place, because your problem may not be your behavior in itself, but the fact that you cannot change your behavior anymore, you cannot control it anymore, you cannot control yourself anymore, not in private and many times not even in society, no matter how much you try. And this is dreadful, because going through life incapable to control yourself must be alarming, since you become rapidly a true menace to yourself and to those around. And this is exactly how people are harmed badly today, losing entire families, dying, or only going to prison indefinitely, in very large numbers.

And once people learn how to control their behavior, they do not have to go through these problems anymore. But can you really control a natural behavior? Besides, the entire judiciary system implemented by society today is not at all meant to recover and remedy social behavior, but it is meant to harm people even more through irrelevant harsh austerity, called punishment. And this harms you, because if society is not capable or is not willing to teach and train you toward your expected behavior and place in society, but only punishes you through its own laws, through its own expectations, within its own environment, and by its own profiteers, then this is not exactly a human world, but a consensual, highly harmful oppressive environment, consensual world meant to harm and even eradicate people. And when you study history, you find out how this has always been the case, all done by one mob of social actors after another.

What can you do, since it seems that you cannot change this world? Can you really not change this world, or this is just another social stereotype? As I always state, change yourself, and this world follows, since this world is only your environment. And if it does not, then too bad for this world.

Have you already tried, and it does not work? Because you have to change your behavior entirely, and at once, by developing entirely from your current first consensual level to the third intelligent human developmental level. Since you can never change your behavior gradually, but only all at once. In other words, you cannot change your behavior one undesired activity at a time, first the wine and beer, and then the cursing and cheating, or maybe the cheating later on eventually, since it will never work. Even more, you cannot change your behavior today, improve your responsibility next year, and then strengthen your reasoning sometimes in the future. Because these are abilities of a same intelligence, they always stand together, and therefore you have to develop them simultaneously. You have to develop the entire intelligence, at once. You have to improve and develop your entire cognitive system, at once. If you know how, because you need all the necessary genuine knowledge about the human behavior, while what sociology, psychology, and education provide today is not enough.

Yet make sure that you know exactly what you should change from your behavior, or you end up harming yourself and your genetic line, while trying to improve. Because some of your 'bad' behavior might actually be good and favorable after all, to remain forbidden and unaccepted by society for various reasons.

For example, your later powerful sexual activity may be considered immoral and perverted through all social norms, it always embarrasses you and you might be charged and punished for it, yet only through your powerful reproductive behavior, you succeed in propagating your own genetic line, which is a highly treasured achievement in life. In a similar manner, your later precognitive, empathic, or telepathic higher behavior may be considered evil, abnormal, unfortunate, dangerous, and satanic by any dogma and social organization out there, yet any higher behavior that you can still manage to undergo today is a significant achievement, mostly after being drugged and indoctrinated strongly your entire life, in every manner. And so you must learn how to distinguish and evaluate on your own all types, elements, and characteristics of your own behavior, in order not to end up harming yourself and those around in the process of discarding your 'bad' behavior while 'improving' yourself.

The question is how to do so, how to improve and develop your behavior. You will not find here a list with what you have to do each day in order to improve your behavior, since this is what ideologies implement, lists of beliefs. Because you have to know all facts about yourself, about society, and about this world, before you can improve in any manner, since there is no other way. As you must always follow your natural higher needs for development.

There are books out there promising you to change any bad behavior in ten days, or in thirty days, through specific meditations or through repeated suggestions, affirmations, repetitive exercises, and various sounds that you can make. If you try them, you get nowhere, because these are based on beliefs, on other people's beliefs about their own current thinking and behavior. And this is how those books may end up changing your beliefs, temporarily or permanently, but not improving your actual behavior. Beliefs may determine and may control your behavior, yet it takes a great effort and a long time of indoctrination to change your behavior through beliefs, while it compromises your entire cognitive system in the process. And if you ever manage to change your behavior through beliefs and dogma, you end up with a copy of someone else's dogma, beliefs, and behavior, which may be consensual, inadequate, and harmful, a behavior of an even lower level than the one you had before. Since dogma is always of the first level, while the intelligent human reasoning and behavior are of the third developmental level, which is the intelligent human level. Because only accurate facts lead to intelligent human reasoning, and then to intelligent human behavior. While beliefs lead to dogma and to ideologies, as these are of the first consensual level. And all that you have to do is study history and sociology to see what dogma, beliefs, and ideologies did to this world throughout time and still do to this world today, while you do not really have to go through all these yourself, and most importantly, you might not want to be part of these.

Are you capable to adjust your behavior as you please, once you manage to live your life at the intelligent human level? Are you capable to control yourself in any manner you desire, including controlling your feelings, bodily appearance, attention, reasoning, and abilities? Well, not really, and not directly, since these are superhuman abilities and behaviors, which are abilities and behaviors of even higher levels. At the intelligent human level, you are capable to understand everything about yourself and your environment, and you are able to use this human knowledge in order to integrate your entire behavior within your various environments: inner and outer, natural and social, objective and subjective. In other words, through an intelligent human behavior, you are capable to stand up and remain above drugs, above servitude, and above all common weakness, ignorance, and incapability. At the intelligent human level, you can control yourself as much as genuinely developed humans are capable to do, since you are capable to maintain the necessary interconnectivity and harmony within your cognitive system and within your immediate society, while always seeking understanding, cooperation, favorable multilateral outcomes, and favorable solutions throughout all your social interactions.

Why exactly do we still encounter these persistent human limitations, and why exactly do you have to be superhuman in order to achieve an entirely consciously controlled behavior? Because you can never control your behavior rigidly and precisely as you drive your car and as you may expect. Because you are not exactly meant to control it, or you are not meant to control it entirely. Because your entire mind generates your needs and your reasoning, needs and reasoning determining now your behavior. While you are not exactly your entire mind. You are only the conscious part of your mind, while you are always responsible with the fulfillment of all needs coming from your entire cognitive system, conscious and subconscious. This is why you cannot control directly your weight, height, bodily temperature, smell, sexual desire, along with your daily digestion and blood pressure, because other intelligences, other cognitive abilities do so throughout your cognitive system. This is their lifelong behavior, to tend to these tasks, and you can never do so in their place. You have to learn these limitations yourself, how and when they occur, why they occur, and more importantly, you have to learn to maintain harmony and cooperation within your inner self, as you must do in the outside world. Because you have to learn to interconnect and integrate your own human behavior within your environment as usefully and as harmoniously as you can. If not, you end up sick, weak, disabled, addicted, confined, meaningless, and unfulfilled, and so you decay.

And this is exactly the kind of knowledge kept away from you throughout life and throughout society, since you are made to believe that you can control your behavior consciously continuously, if you only desire it strongly, and if you can train yourself. But you cannot. You may still cooperate within your cognitive system and within your social environment, and therefore you can manage to influence these toward a common goal. But you cannot do even this, unless you know everything about yourself and about your environment, and therefore unless you manage to interconnect and integrate yourself perfectly in your environment, cognitive and social, to maintain your lifelong harmony there. Which you cannot, since there is no discipline in society knowing and teaching this accurate knowledge, so you remain ignorant, and therefore you remain on lower behavioral levels. And so you end up failing continuously in life, this stops you from developing, it forces you to behave at lower developmental levels and on consensual, enforced modes of life, and you can do nothing about it. Just look around to notice how people achieve to live their lives at the intelligent human level, and you understand society and the entire world for what they truly are. Because this is not exactly a human society, while what you see around are not exactly human behaviors. And this is the problem, by far worse than you walking around your bedroom naked.

And after all these, society judges and punishes you now for the behavior that you have to undergo naturally on behalf of both your conscious and subconscious mind. And since many of your needs coming from your subconscious mind remain forbidden and taboo in society today, good luck to you. Because your subconscious will never cease to send you these 'bad,' 'guilty,' and 'shameful' needs, while you suppress them as much as you can. So brace yourself, because you still have to find a way to fulfill these, eventually. And this is how you end up dissociating your behavior into your beautifully polished façade that you carry around in society, and into the carefully hidden shadow that you become in privacy. Incredibly, this form of behavioral dissociation has become the accepted norm for the human behavior, and it is even encouraged implicitly.

And this is how you have to live your life now, if you are still at a lower developmental level. And it might be designed by society on purpose to happen in this manner, for you to be guilty, to feel guilty, and to fail in life, by default, through your own needs, reasoning, and behavior, and through your own limitations, natural and consensual.

What defines being human is the capability to control yourself consciously, the capability to dominate your subconscious through your conscious mind. Yet what society expects from you is to be able to control your subconscious directly, entirely, rigidly, in all instances, just as it desires, and just as it controls you continuously through its severe laws.

And it does not work, because you are an intelligent living human being, and not a mechanism, because you have your own normal natural needs and meanings, and you cannot simply turn them on and off to match the rapid succession of laws and social norms throughout history and throughout this world.

Yet who can see this hidden problem today, in a world full of people interested mostly in drugs and material values? Because if you want to understand yourself, first you have to understand this world. You can never understand your behavior entirely by considering it separately from everybody else's behavior, and this is why you have to study society, along with all its social classes and layers. You have to study the human mind, including all its intelligences and cognitive interconnectivity. You have to study your actual environment, along with all its niches and conditions. You have to study life itself, with all its living classes and continuous development, along with much more.

This learning behavior is called living your life at the third level, which is the intelligent human level. It is a third level human behavior that you undergo right now while reading this book, and you do so through your third level human reasoning, while fulfilling your third level human needs. And you are even rewarded for it greatly, with higher level happiness and fulfillment.

What defines society at the level of its lowest social class, at the level of the Masses, is that while the Masses are sabotaged and therefore determined continuously to remain underdeveloped through all means, in order to remain below the human developmental level, the Masses are also expected through social norms and social laws to behave at the intelligent human level, which may be technically impossible. And so the Masses are monitored, caught, charged, judged, and punished accordingly, for any mistake that they make, and for any failure that they manifest. And since most of the visible society consists of the Masses, this may be your case. If you fail to develop and control yourself consciously and continuously throughout life, you end up underdeveloped, undergoing a dissociated behavior, breaking laws and getting caught, being judged and getting punished, all through human laws, allowed by all higher authorities, while you feel guilty and ashamed for what you do, and you blame it on yourself.

And this is the case with everybody, just because you can never obey all human laws continuously, through a lower level behavior, since it is naturally impossible. In real life, consciousness may supervise and dominate the subconscious mind through intelligent human reasoning and behavior, but it does so only temporarily, and only as long as you are at work, at school, or in society in general. While this is exactly why you have to switch to your private life daily, for hours in a row, only to be able to fulfill the rest of your natural needs, the unaccepted ones. To do so in peace, to be able to undergo your burden, your shadow behavior.

The two upper social classes, the Brotherhood and the Elite, behave similarly, since they have similar needs, despite of what they may claim. Only that justice tends to address and charge the Masses but not the Brotherhood and not the Elite, and so these are free to behave as they please. And with the Masses tending diligently to their consensual needs, the Brotherhood and the Elite are free to behave as they please. While keeping not only their behavior hidden from the rest of society, but many times, by keeping their entire existence hidden. And so an entire world is forced now to live in hypocrisy, only because someone had decided how much and at what pace humans should be allowed to develop, what laws should be implemented in society, what natural behavior is allowed and what is bad, and what may be real in this world and what may be false.

What can you do? Seek to develop to the intelligent human level, and do so comprehensively, because it does not work otherwise, and you risk decaying to your lower levels. Because only at the third level, which is the intelligent human level, you are able to distinguish between the consensual and the accurate.

What exactly will justice do when all drugs become legal? Will justice go to every inmate that it had imprisoned for months and years now, to excuse itself for implementing a dreadful punishment that is not in effect anymore because rules change? Is this a game? 'You were never bad, so here you go, you are free now, bye-bye, after three years in prison.' Can bad behaviors be bad only on Tuesdays and Thursdays, while they are good and widely accepted the rest of the time? For what meaning? Because this is the difference between the consensual and the accurate. And why do people always have to suffer in mass for someone else's idiocy, mostly when this idiocy happens to control society? Do you see now the difference between the genuinely bad behavior and the legally, consensually, or socially bad behavior?

Are these social laws nothing else but a constructed regulator meant to control you while fulfilling someone's interests and agenda? And now, whenever you break these invented consensual laws through your natural behavior, natural behavior that you have to undergo while fulfilling your natural needs, you have to pay fines, to go to prison, or to lose your family, indefinitely.

What exactly distinguishes good behaviors from bad ones if authorities change laws continuously, contradicting themselves throughout time, repeatedly? Even more, why exactly are you not allowed to decide for yourself what is good and what is bad in life, but to listen to this contradiction? Whatever it is, it always relates with authorities, with what authorities decide for you to do, and more importantly, it relates with you having to recognize these authorities. And now, you cannot live your life without them, you cannot behave freely and naturally without them, ruining your life in the process, compromising your meaning in life, while harming the human environment.

Yet there are other questions here that you should consider besides what is good and bad in this world. What is real and what is unreal in this world? How much of this world is what it seems and how much is illusory? What is truly allowed and what is forbidden to do in this world? What laws are truly accurate, and what laws are harmful on purpose, meant only to keep you busy and distracted? What knowledge is actually true and what is erroneous in this world?

If you only knew these answers, you could manage to live your life at higher developmental levels, yet this is not always the case. Because you achieve to live your life at the intelligent human level, only if you do not turn to a specifically designated discipline or authority to give you these answers, authority dictating to you in this manner what is good and what is bad in life, what is true and what is false in this world, and what is allowed and what is forbidden in society. Since only then, you manage to be independent in life, to reason for yourself, and to behave in concordance with your true meaning. Because independent reasoning free of dogmas and false beliefs ensures an independent behavior, while freedom defines genuinely developed humans the most.

We already notice a specific line of causality outlining our model for the human behavior: your needs are the ones determining your actions and your entire behavior throughout life, consciously or not, willingly or not, line of causality determining and regulating in this manner your entire behavior. In fact, everything that you do in life you do in order to fulfill your needs and meanings, and this is your behavior. These needs may be natural, as your physiological needs, or they may be consensual in nature, as needs generated by any dogma, stereotype, jurisdiction, hierarchy, and ideology. You should be able to distinguish among your natural and consensual needs, since the behaviors that these generate are natural and consensual, and many times, adequate or inadequate. Whatever the case is, everything that you do in life, your entire behavior has one meaning, to fulfill your needs, along with your family's needs, along with your social needs, along with your higher needs, since all needs are of various types and they come on various levels and classes.

As stated previously, needs determine your behavior, and not the other way around. Which means that, throughout your lifeline of causality, your needs precede your behavior, they are the cause of your behavior, and therefore your needs must be addressed first whenever you try to change your behavior. Or this remains the case if there is nothing else preceding your needs to become your main cause.

Needs are not the only elements preceding and therefore determining your behavior, but your reasoning is caused by your needs, while your reasoning determines your behavior directly. The causal order so far is: needs and meanings, determining your reasoning, determining your behavior. Because most of the time, you have to reason hard in order to find a way to fulfill your needs and meanings.

And this is how you may construct your behavior, one procedure at a time. You have to feel hunger first, which is your need for food, and then you start reasoning intensely, in order to figure out the best way to get the best food at the fresh market, in the easiest and in the least expensive manner. You undergo this entire buying and feeding model in your mind, by taking your imagination from food stand to food stand, from food item to food item, from nutrient to nutrient, and even from one outcome to another, modeling or predicting what consequences all these may have on your vibrancy and wellbeing. Once everything seems acceptable, plausible, and successful enough in your mind, then you do everything in the real world. You start your actual physical behavior, you go to buy your precise food from the precise stand and you take it at your little table, to eat it there. And this is your comprehensive behavior, cognitive in nature at first or subjective, and then physical in nature or objective. And this is exactly how you always reason, through mental models, and this is how your hunger develops to become your feeding behavior for the day. And if this is always successful, it becomes your normal behavior for life, having your lunch directly at the fresh market, since it becomes your routine.

As another example, when you happen to feel bored and you have plenty of time to spare, you identify first your boredom as your higher need for learning, and not as your lower need for entertainment. You think hard and then you find a highly useful learning material, a podcast, a book, or a website, and so you start learning, about the human behavior, and so you read this book. And this is your learning behavior for today, an intelligent human behavior. And you should undergo intelligent human activities every day, since you receive your higher needs every day. Since without them, your life feels empty.

You may always check how adequate your current behavior is, by the type and amount of happiness that you receive, by the intensity of this happiness, and by its texture. Because your behavior is continuously regulated intrinsically, through your punishment-reward cognitive mechanism, or through pleasure-pain, satisfaction-boredom, or love-hate, depending on your needs, fulfillment, timing, and rate of success. The specific amplitude, texture, or consistency in your feelings inform you of the specific neurotransmitters sending you the pleasure or pain, information leading all the way to your meaning in life. While this type of knowledge and continuous reasoning and self-monitoring are typical in any intelligent human behavior, which may be objective, social, cognitive, or interconnective.

These were simple examples, yet life and the environment can become highly demanding at times. If you happen to scream at your daughter or punish her in any manner whenever you catch her smoking, you do so in order to make her stop smoking at once, induce a good behavior to last her a lifetime, and make you proud as a parent. Yet what you end up doing is simply attempting to address a symptom, an effect, which is the act of smoking itself, while stronger, more relevant causes had already preceded this behavior throughout her lifeline of causality, as her reasoning, meaning in life, environment, and motivation, along with social needs of various levels, and along with many other causes generating and influencing these, determining her to smoke right now, when you caught her. You must always go for the main cause itself and fix that, if you are ever capable to find it throughout tedious lifelines of causality. Because addressing effects and symptoms, while attempting to change unfavorable or inadmissible behaviors, will give you no results at all, but will only waste your time, hopes, and effort, while ruining priceless relationships in the process.

Needs are not main casual elements throughout lifelines of causality, since someone or something has to send you these needs first, for you to fulfill now throughout your behavior. Your subconscious sends you your needs throughout life, physiological and social needs mostly. Your subconscious mind is composed of many cognitive abilities, as your eating, recovery, or social abilities. In fact, you the conscious intelligence are simply just another ability of your cognitive system. You are the ability of your organism to interact with the outside world in a conscious manner. You are responsible with the actual behavior of your organism in the outside world, while it fulfills all needs. You call yourself conscious just because you are capable to identify yourself as being conscious, which you always are. All intelligences are conscious, but since you cannot reach, access, and therefore identify directly the other intelligences of your cognitive system, you cannot observe their consciousness directly, and therefore you cannot state that they are conscious or not. And this is how you call yourself the conscious intelligence, while you refer to the rest of your mind as being your subconscious. Which sounds amusing, now when you consider it.

These inner cognitive abilities, or cognitive entities, or intelligences, manage the entire inner activity throughout your brain and body. These are the intelligences sending you your needs, everything from hunger to fear, determination for social interaction, recovery, sexual desire, learning, development, equality, or revenge.

We will study needs and intelligences, along with the entire cognitive system in the second chapter of this book, since these are highly relevant in determining and controlling your behavior. And if you want to change your behavior, you have to change your reasoning, beliefs, attitudes, and stereotypes first, and many times, you have to reach the deepest corners of your subconscious mind in order to do so and solve your cognitive problems, for your entire lifeline of causality to resettle properly, and therefore to determine a stable, long-lasting, favorable behavior. While is not as difficult as it seems.

And then, preceding these primal intelligences from your own lifeline of causality, there is the environment itself, your natural, objective, inner, ideal, subjective, cognitive, online, higher, and social environments, all forming your environment. Your environment demands everything from you endlessly, and you always have to consider it, only to be able to fulfill your needs. Your environment forces you to engage it and cope with it, or else you suffer, you fail, or you die. This causes in this manner your entire lifeline of causality to happen and manifest just it does, leading to your continuous, consistent, never ceasing behavior, which represents now your own, personal, and unique existence, along with your own identity and existential status, along with your own rights. And these should be at the same level, hopefully at the third intelligent level, if you strive and claim to live your life at the intelligent human level.

All these causal elements happen to be at the same level, since this is the developmental level of your own intelligence. Because these are characteristics, abilities, behaviors, tendencies, results, and byproducts of your own intelligence. We study all elements found on your lifeline of causality in separate chapters, since they lead to your temporary or lifelong behavior. Our model for the human behavior gains new perspectives now, the environmental and existential perspectives, adding to our social, cognitive, ideal, dogmatic, and empiric perspectives, among others that we will encounter and consider throughout the book.

Do you see why you have to understand the behavior of all human beings from all social classes, hidden or not, in order to understand your own behavior, before attempting to change and improve it in any manner? Do you see how you have to understand the behavior of your students and children first, along with their entire environment, before attempting to educate them?

And this is why now every time you stop eating in order to lose weight, you end up gaining weight, because your normal eating behavior does not cause you to change your bodily weight, just because your physical act of eating cannot affect your bodily weight on a longer term. Your subconscious mind is the one managing your digestion, nutrient distribution, and food storage as fat within your body, while you engage in your eating activity because of your need for food that you receive from your subconscious. You simply do as you are told. While your subconscious has to cope with your natural and social environments, matching and providing what energy and nutrients your environment will demand from you that day, that week, or that entire year. Because ever since you have started this insane diet, your subconscious has to cope with you. And judging by all statistics, the subconscious always wins, making you eat not only what you have to eat normally, but it forces you now to eat everything, while it stores everything as fat throughout your body, in case that you ever decide to stop eating again.

Your subconscious sends you hunger, which is the need for food, while you the conscious intelligence receive this need, and you have to interact with the outside world in order to fulfill it, by actually eating whatever you desire, and in whatever amount you desire. But it is not you desiring the entire time even though it feels this way through your own hunger, but it is the subconscious intelligence desiring it. This is exactly what the subconscious demands from you through your feelings, and it does so all the way down to the last molecule of nutrient, since it is very precise. Your subconscious also digests the food not through bulk chemical reactions, but it handles the food and nutrients molecule by molecule, and then it sends it to every cell of your body exactly as they demand, down to the last molecule.

This entire eating activity is very precise, and therefore you must be just as precise when you eat. This is why, if you happen to use a scale to weight every piece of cheese before you eat it in order to control your bodily weight because you saw this on the Internet and they even give you there a list with all the numbers and nutrients for you to lose weight fast. While you do not know what you do, because the human body is by far more complex than your scale and list. Because you already have your natural need for food and you cannot parallel it with your list. The food that you eat is meant to provide energy and nutrients for the successful behavior of zillions of cells and cellular components that all happen to be unique, they have unique needs and they undergo their own unique behavior, and if you keep interfering with their life, their tasks, and their behavior, this is exactly how you are harmed.

Just follow your natural needs and feelings, because these are very precise, and with a little reasoning and cooperation from your part, you will manage to interconnect with your subconscious mind, understand its cognitive behavior, do your part, maintain your inner harmony, and therefore you achieve to maintain yourself good looking, healthy, vibrant, and in very good shape.

Because there are many other elements on your specific lifeline of causality determining your eating behavior besides your sudden idea of stopping eating today. You should know them, or your own eating behavior becomes inadequate, and it disturbs your inner and outer equilibrium.

Why the complexity? Life becomes tedious, many times not exactly because you have to fulfill tedious needs, but because you have to fulfill them alongside millions or billions of people. Life certainly improves when you manage to interconnect with them through who they are and not through what they do for you, because then you keep the harmony among yourselves, and therefore you manage to interact lovingly and constructively with each other. And then, life becomes more complex when you consider the zillions of living components of your own organism and cognitive system, as your cells and cellular components, along with all your intelligences, since they are alive, and you may always interconnect with them, to form and maintain a similarly loving, constructive harmony.

And now you understand why simply by screaming at your daughter will never help her with her smoking behavior, but will only distance her from you, because her specific lifeline of causality is very crowded right now when it comes to smoking, since she already feels more socially insecure at school. And by engaging in all grownup activities that she can find, it should strengthen her social status, her social acceptance, or this is what she expects. This is what she came up with, because smoking worked well with many of her colleagues, and they are well accepted at school by now. They are strong, so strong in all entourages, that they can afford to get on her case, continuously. And she is the last one in school now, the weakest, the black sheep, and if you only knew how dreadful her life is now at school, that she actually had to choose between smoking and suicide. And even now, smoking barely works, she hangs on to life by a last thread, if you only knew, then you would have thought better before you screamed at her. And now, with your latest behavior, it seems that she is losing you, the one to have cared for her the most, the one to have understood her the most. You would have thought better, if you only knew.

But why do all these have to happen even today, in our developed society, in our advanced civilization? This is certainly an abnormal behavior taking place within the school environment, since everything that is not normal today has to be abnormal. Psychology, sociology, and education label everyone involved in this case with abnormal behavior, since if it was normal behavior, then all these students were at their desks even during recession, learning hard. And this is exactly the problem, because society with all its disciplines and authorities fails to interconnect with the people. Society and authorities simply construct your expected behavior out of nothing, in its most consensual and inadequate state, and now they expect you to follow this consensually constructed behavior diligently, while most of it interacts harmfully with the normal, natural behavior assumed by your subconscious mind. And if you cannot do what society wants from you, if you refuse to do so, if you become bored and restless, if you do something else or if you fall behind, then you are considered aggressive, sick, abnormal, hyperactive, or dyslexic, and so you are doomed to remain labeled with mental sicknesses, at the mercy of psychiatry and medicine for life. And what a life.

Now the students involved in this incident are labeled with addictive, suicidal, and aggressive behavior, psychology addresses them with counseling sessions and medication that may end up harming them even more, because psychology and medicine attempt to cure effects, symptoms, and even entire behaviors with drugs, leaving the main causes to persist.

What main causes exactly? It is not hard to find them, mostly when you have been a parent or a teacher for some time. But why exactly does it have to happen in this manner? Because behaviorism and cognitivism fail to offer an accurate model for the human mind and human behavior. And they fail in this manner in all instances, not only here. Because the main factors controlling, deciding, and regulating behaviors in general are never considered by psychology, sociology, and education. And these are the media and entertainment, among many others found all over your lifeline of causality now, determining and controlling your attitudes and behavior. If you happen to see drugs and violence in the news and in entertainment every minute, be sure that you find drugs and violence in schools, because students and teachers bring them there, through their behavior.

Schools currently address very few cases of violence, only the most obvious ones. And this is just another hypocrisy, since violence and addictions are found and manifest in everybody's behavior, knowingly or not, willingly or not, since everybody lives in the same environment and is affected by the same environment, not only bullies, addicts, and victims. Everyone is alike today, nobody is better or worse throughout society, only that some people are worse than others at handling and hiding their shadow behavior. These are the ones being caught usually, and now, an entire society turns around to condemn them dreadfully, to harass them with punishment and banishment by law, by their law, managing in this manner to hide better their own shadows, their own 'bad' behavior. Why not accepting them, while they have the chance to identify and control their behavior? Because when you manage to know them for who they really are, you find out that they are not bad people, but good. You find out how rejection, drugs, stereotypes, and violence in the environment cause them to become violent themselves, while this may happen to anyone including your children, and to you.

We may go even further on your lifeline of causality while finding the main causes determining your behavior. Who exactly puts drugs and violence in the media and in entertainment? Because environments may remain the main cause for your behavior, but environments may also be altered and controlled, as they may be consensually constructed in order to generate in you and in your children specific behaviors, good or bad, depending on cases. Because it is never someone up there at the top of society controlling you and your loved ones closely and directly, as you learn from conspiracy theories, but there are only some capable public relators working hard in the background to alter your environment in every manner, in order to determine you to behave according to the orders that they receive from above. Consequently, nobody actually harasses and oppresses the people of this world, but the people of this world harass and oppress each other, just by having to live a lifetime in this altered, harmful, dry, consensual environment.

Nobody censors and regulates your behavior, but you regulate your own behavior yourself. While you harm yourself in the process, even badly, through your own free agreement. And you do so only to be able to integrate in your environment, only to be socially accepted there, and only to become more socially competitive, because you will always turn around to do to others whatever the others do to you. Not because you are bad, sick, or abnormal yourself, since nobody is, but because there is no other way, it is part of everyone's life, it is part of the social race, since it is the only environment that everybody has, and it is unnatural and harmful. And it is a hard race going on out there in this world, with you being caught right in the middle, engaging you and taking you to your limits. And this is your behavior, for life.

And examples can go on indefinitely, since it is important to cover the human needs, the human reasoning, and the human environment, along with society and those controlling you and your behavior, how they do so and with what intentions, along with many other significant factors.

2 YOUR INTERCONNECTIVE SOCIAL BEHAVIOR

This entire model is very complex, since the human behavior is the most tedious concept to model and understand. In itself, the human behavior is the most complex existential structure in this world. Or maybe the human brain, the human mind, and the human body must be the most complex structures in the known universe, not the human behavior, which seems rather abstract. I have actually modeled these too in separate books of this series, and in comparison with the human behavior, these are but simple elements on a lifeline of causality, converging to a single result, a single meaning, the human behavior. Because when you model the human behavior, you must include human needs, human meanings, human environment, human reasoning, human potential, human interconnectivity, society, control, conspiracies, causality, along with the entire world, with entire models done for all the people in this world including you, because you superimpose through all your lifelines of causality, since all lifelines of causality are interconnected, they are one.

And as you notice, the human behavior is by far the most complex, the most tedious to mental model. While we have to make this model with no help from science, since science stands in concealment, in dogma, and in ignorance throughout highly important topics. What is the universe? How exactly does the human mind reason? What is the meaning of life? 'We don't know yet,' science answers with its entire army of millions of scientists. But then, what exactly do you know? What exactly do you do there the entire time? 'We don't know, yet.'

I will maintain this first part of this book empiric, studying here your physical and social behavior, while covering here environment, society, social classes, social niches, interconnectivity, causality, Life, and existence. Needs and reasoning influencing behavior are cognitive and therefore subjective in nature, and I cover them later on.

And if you are still comparing in your mind the complexity of this model with the model for the Deity, you may consider that Life, causality, Intelligence, and existence address directly the Deity, just as they address directly all living beings and their behavior, and this includes humans and the human behavior. Even more, the human behavior in itself defines and becomes direct integral part of the Deity itself, just because the Deity is everything everywhere ever, including you, your environment, and your behavior. Because it is your behavior influencing and contributing directly to this world and to everything that exists objectively, subjectively, and highjectively.

You are your behavior since your behavior counts in this world and how this world perceives and understands you. But this is not the case entirely, since you are also who you are, the intelligent living human being, since many times, your loved ones love you more for who you are and not for what you do for them. Let us study here behavior versus living nature, since it leads to an important type of behavior, the natural, intelligent human interconnective behavior.

It is up to you how much you contribute to this world through who you are, and how much you contribute to this world through what you do. Yet this dissociated contribution counts for this world depending on your developmental level, and depending on the developmental level of this world. From your own perspective, you are certainly who you are, while you are less what you do in this world. What exactly does your behavior mean for you? You certainly care for yourself, for your family, for society, and for the entire world. But many times, when you brush your teeth, or when you take the bus, when you dust the sofa and when you tie your shoelaces, your behavior seems to be something that you have to do anyway throughout the day, you have always been doing so, and many times, you do not even realize it, and you do not care much about, for as long as you fulfill your duties, your needs, and your meanings in life.

For this world in general, your behavior is all that you do, just because this is what this world can see and identify from your part, technically. Maybe this is the case because you are one among billions as you, or maybe this is the case because the entire world is designed to be in this manner, resembling farms, factories, plantations, prisons, and military camps, where all living beings are units, concepts, and principles but not living beings, all having numbers and designations but not names and hearts, all having laws and duties but not freedom and love, all standing vulnerable, but not interconnected.

What exactly is interconnective behavior, and what can it ever do to this world? It is everything and it should be always present in this world, unless living beings become consensually disconnected. And when all people disconnect, there is no more love, all problems start, life becomes dry and empty, you try to compensate with drugs and possessions, you disconnect even more from Life, and so you cannot control your behavior anymore. Because behaviors were meant to be pieces of life, while consensual behaviors are not alive but dead, consensually dead. Because Life is structured into classes of life everywhere, and this is why living interconnectivity is a natural tendency, a natural need, a natural effect, and it should be active part in the behavior of all living beings. You may remain interconnected with your family and friends for life, you call them your loved ones, but you were supposed to remain interconnected with everybody else, since classes of life are comprehensive. But you do not, and neither does everybody else.

We take an example here to understand the consensual behavior and the living nature, as seen from the outside world, from society. Because from your own inner perspective, there is a difference between your living nature and your behavior, between who you are and what you do, and between you as an intelligent living human being and the specific consensual spot that you occupy in society. It is easier to see this difference from within than from the outside world, so let us see the example.

You decided to hire a house cleaner to come daily and clean the house. Genuinely developed humans do not let others tend to their physiological needs, out of respect, but you are determined now to hire a so-called domestic, since your ex-husband pays for it anyway. She started this week, she comes to clean the house every day, and it is a great help. While for you, your house cleaner is the specialization that she occupies in society, she cleans up people's houses, she makes an income, and she provides in this manner for her family. It is a normal job just as yours, behaving normally as everybody else.

But then when she got sick, you hired an older woman, then a college student, and then several months later, you had to hire a newly arrived immigrant, since you could not find anyone else and you needed something fast. For you, you never care for their living nature, for who they are, but only for the job that they do, and it is very helpful and very convenient. And they seem to work the same anyway, all domestics do, and the house is always clean.

But then, your hours changed at work, allowing you to start work one hour later. And so you had to stay home every morning, with the house cleaner. For one entire hour. It seemed awkward at first, for both of you, but then you learned that she has two children the same age as yours, two beautiful boys, and she showed you the pictures. You recommended her a good car model, one that you used to have long ago and it is very affordable today, while you learned how to arrange your shelves prettier. Then one day, she helped you cook her favorite stew, and the children just loved it. At no extra cost. And then you started being more careful in the kitchen and in the bathroom throughout the day, not to mess up the house too much, and you taught the children to do the same. And then throughout the summer vacation, she brought her children with her, to swim in the pool. And they were adorable. Your children played with them, and the house felt so happy and harmonious while they were there, every morning. And your house cleaner was not exactly a house cleaner anymore, but she was Rebecca, you loved her and the children loved her, and you did everything you could to keep her, because she was unique, priceless, irreplaceable, she was Rebecca.

Why dissociating and discriminating among people? Why should those around count for you as who they really are, and be more privileged than anyone else? Note that at home, in private, you form your own miniature society, a buffer between you and the actual current consensual human society, private living human society that you may have in any form and at any developmental level that you need. The great majority of families are private miniature living human societies, and when you study them closely, you find them at the third, intelligent human level. And when your family or immediate entourage are developed, then all members behave at higher developmental levels, since they are allowed to do so. It is there and then that you consider everyone around as who they are, the intelligent living human beings, and not as what they do for you and the rest of this world.

Because this is the difference between the third level intelligent human society and the current first level consensual society, since one is alive while the other is dead, consensually dead, and part of the Consensual Matrix. Because the intelligent human society was supposed to be a comprehensive human family spanning this world, similar to the little family that you have at home, since your family is your own, intelligent human family that you are allowed to have in private, at home, and it is of the third, intelligent human level.

While the intelligent human society is erased today, systematically, by the Consensual Matrix, through the multitude of consensual orders, duties, and assignments that you fulfill continuously, leaving behind the current first level consensual human society.

And as you notice, you do so to yourself, and everybody does the same, since everybody fulfills consensual duties. And now, this is the world you live in, this is the difference between your living social identity and what you do for the consensual world, which is your consensual self, or your brand, trademark, or consensual corporation, undergoing its existence in the Consensual Matrix. And this is your existence, consensual, since you undergo it mostly through your consensual self throughout life, which is actually your corporation.

What is the difference between families and society? Society is of the first consensual level, entirely controlled, while families are of the third intelligent developmental level. Society should be of the third intelligent developmental level as well, as a large family, yet it is kept instated consensually, against Life, for various reasons.

Should people divorce society and live individually from now on? No, not at all. But people should live in a third level intelligent human society, just because humans are third level intelligent living beings, they are living human beings. While humans are developed at the third level naturally, through their extraordinary mind and reasoning. Even more, members of all classes of life should be able to live life at the third developmental level and not at the first, because this is why classes of Life form, to allow them to live life at the third intelligent human level.

And this is why this world is a stage, a Consensual Matrix, where people contribute with their consensual behavior, with their role that they are, as actors do. They take their orders, they work eight hours a day and five days a week, they bring a profit and they acquire the goods, they take their drugs and they teach others to do the same, they follow the laws and they suffer the pain, they dry up this world and they suffer the same, they diverge from Life and their own life diverges out of control, and out of tune. What exactly is the meaning in life? Hopefully not this.

Why would Life ever allow a significant class of life, the human society, to exist at the first, dead, consensual level, with everybody inside disconnected, in hierarchic bondage, while seeking pleasure but not harmony, human fulfillment, and love? And this is exactly the question now, because this is exactly why your life feels many times, dry, irrelevant, and out of control, affecting your behavior accordingly. The reason is that you cannot have pleasure and happiness simultaneously, just because pleasure is addictive, while happiness is not. You cannot have pleasure and love simultaneously, for the same reason. You cannot have drugs and happiness simultaneously, and you cannot have material and selfish interests along with love. There is a great conflict taking place here, between the natural and the consensual, and you must know what exactly triggers it, under what circumstances, and with what effects.

And just because the human society is made by intelligent beings, this does not mean that it should be consensual and out of concordance with Life, because it should not. What happens is that the entire human environment is kept consensual on purpose, as in a matrix, for various reasons, but mostly in order to remain compatible with the overall Consensual Matrix spanning most of the wider world in all its realities, and this causes people to be and remain disconnected throughout life, maintaining this consensual environment themselves, and consequently having to undergo a consensual, inadequate behavior. And this is your problem, right here. While you can never leave your consensual environment, because you hold it instated yourself, you hold it instated through your own consensual behavior, through your own agreement.

Let us cover briefly developmental levels now. These apply to classes of life and to individual living beings, since you can never distinguish between classes and individual beings. Humans may be considered individuals, yet humans are entire classes of life in themselves, being composed of cells and cellular components, while all these are classes of life in themselves when studied closely.

Zero level societies are made of dysfunctional individuals, as very sick, very disabled, or very addicted.

Moving to the first level, individuals of a first level society work in servitude their entire life and this is why they are only what they do for this world, before they die. And this is why their behavior is everything that matters within first level societies, and nothing else.

Second level societies are groups of animals gathered together, as herds and packs, with individuals fulfilling needs throughout life in every manner, engaging in win-win or win-lose interactions intuitively, while no one seems to care if they harm others in the process. Who you are and what you do matters less within second level societies, as long as you manage to fulfill your needs, before you die.

Third level societies are intelligent human societies, made of individuals determined to engage only in win-win circumstances throughout their entire social interaction, through their entire behavior, explicit or implicit. Individuals of a third level society represent both who they are and what they do in this world, since they are both the actors and the intelligent living beings behind their social specialization and social meaning.

Higher level societies allow members to identify themselves with their living nature, as societies of angels, which are of the fourth and fifth levels, along with societies of Free Spirits, which are of the seventh level.

In general, you seek to match your own developmental level with the level of your society, and with the level of your entire environment. Societies of a level lower than yours will cause your rapid decay, while societies of a higher level than yours can help you ascend in development. It is important to state here that since lifelines of causality relate to individuals, to their environment, to their intelligence, to their society, and to their behavior, it is important that all these, along with everything caused and determined by them, must remain at the same correspondent number, which happens to be the number three for genuinely developed humans. Otherwise, you live a lifetime disconnected and in disequilibrium, and you decay. And since society is always at the first consensual servitude level, you are doomed to remain at the first consensual servitude level. Yet you can still find pockets of developed people in this world, and you could manage to move there and live among them. Or you emigrate to another country that may seem to be higher in development, and when you get there, you realize that everything is the same, part of the same consensual society.

Societies are classes of life in themselves, and they should always remain classes of life, since they are composed of individual living beings. Cells are a class of life in themselves, yet cells have gathered to form a class of life of an even higher level, which is the organism. Organisms gather to form classes of life of even higher levels, which are herds, packs, societies, civilizations, and then worlds, realities, and clusters of realities, one class level after another, up to Life herself.

The reason why living beings gather to live life within societies, forming therefore classes of life of higher levels, is to be able to live life at a higher developmental level. And they do so because their capabilities do not allow it individually. And this makes a tremendous difference, because as a class, they are capable to cope with the environment better than they could before.

What is the strategy of this extraordinary achievement? All members of any class of life must remain continuously interconnected, in a living, natural manner, as families offer today. Cells remain within organisms endlessly, while cellular components remain within their cells endlessly, all being interconnected, all behaving harmoniously. Everybody must tend to everybody through their individual life and through their specific meaning, ability, and specialization without exception, and so they do. Since they have their specific needs and feelings allowing them to do so, and through these, they are able to undergo the most adequate and the most harmonious behavior, tending in this manner to the entire class of life. And it is natural, it is alive. While everything remains in this manner at the third intelligent level within all classes of life: behavior, lifestyle, inner environment, needs, thinking, interaction, interconnectivity, feelings, development, and fulfillment.

When you study cells, you find them interconnected, harmonious, and efficient, so harmonious and so efficient, that you may consider them individual living beings, and not entire living communities.

And now, what is the problem with classes of life? When one member fails, when one specialization or ability fails, then the entire class of life fails, becoming harmed, sick, disabled, and compromised. Or it may even die, only for one domain, specialization, capability, or sometimes only for one individual living being. And this is exactly why all living beings have to remain entirely interconnected within classes of life and therefore entirely harmonious, just as humans remain interconnected continuously within their families. Because if one fails, everybody fails.

And therefore, this is the problem with the current society, humans remain interconnected only within their families, but not within the rest of society. And this is why many fail throughout life, while the rest of this world never cares, with the entire society, suffering consequently, including all families.

You might consider that the rich control everything, yet this is not true. Because the rich cannot control the next cataclysm. And if one of those individuals who was killed or left to die was supposed to provide the accurate solution for how avoid the next cataclysm along with all the future similar ones, then the entire class of life dies, which is the human society. Because this is why Life provides the necessary genetic diversity within classes, in order to allow their survival to be of a very high level. Yet with an interconnectivity below level three, you end up losing your genetic diversity in every manner, and the entire class dies, which is the human society. Yet it is not the only civilization in the wider world going extinct, so Life goes on, without humans.

And why does it happen? Because no one cares about any of these, since everybody is disconnected, while care implies interconnectivity. People have other interests in life, as making money, buying things, being entertained, or taking drugs, all being selfish, and many times going against society altogether. And you cannot have drugs and knowledge simultaneously throughout life, as you cannot have selfish interests and social achievements, since these are mutually exclusive. Since this disconnects this world, and this is why society resembles today to an extraordinary funeral march taking everybody to the common grave.

Societies are living classes of life, and they go up to the tenth supreme level, as all intelligences, worlds, and civilizations do. Life, Intelligence, and the wider world are of the tenth level, as being everything, everyone, everywhere, ever. Right below Life, there are the interconnected intelligences, these ninth level intelligences capable to remain interconnected with Life and therefore with the entire wide world indefinitely. These ninth level intelligences undergo an interconnective behavior continuously, along with their normal subjective and highjective behaviors. However, this specific interconnective behavior in itself is nothing else than your specific interconnective behavior that you had with Rebecca, when you distinguished between her as a living human being and her as a house cleaner.

Because it is not only a social interconnection linking all members of a society, but it is a loving interconnection in parallel with it, exactly as it takes place within families. And this was supposed to be the case for the entire society, but people made a mockery of this world, by using money, orders, ideologies, privileged political parties, and consensual hierarchies within, disregarding love and human nature entirely. And now, whenever people try to interconnect naturally among themselves, they are stopped, killed, accused, and prosecuted.

Because society is maintained in its consensual state

deliberately, always at the first servitude level. It is maintained in this manner by people themselves, thorough their behavior, the same consensual behavior that makes you feel empty in life, meaningless, and out of control. Or this is the case when you step outside your family and private life because it is a jungle out there, so don't forget to lock the door.

What exactly defines this interconnective behavior, what triggers it, and how exactly can you control it consciously throughout life? Genuinely developed humans have the capability to undergo interconnective behaviors. All animals do, but not all people. Because various chemical additives destroy the specific areas and glands of the body and brain meant to assure genuine cognitive interconnectivity within the human mind, and through it, meant to assure higher consciousness and higher reasoning, along with the rest of the higher cognitive abilities.

Cognitive interconnectivity means direct interconnection through the mind of every kind. In itself, cognitive interconnectivity is a highjective behavior, a behavior that you undergo through your higher self, which represents the higher side of your mind, your highconscious. The cognitive interconnectivity is the ability for two or more living beings or intelligences to interconnect in one mind, to be part of a same class of life, in a highjective manner.

People are interconnected in society, yet they are interconnected at a lower level. Money motivates and interconnects people today, while money is capable to determine people to sustain and maintain the entire human civilization exactly as it is today, which may be considered a significant achievement, but not entirely. Because all dreadful news that you see on TV are part of the consensual civilization, and they are caused by money and by material possessions, not by social achievements. Money, orders, and laws, should assure a second level interconnectivity in society, but through direct social control, money, orders, and laws enforce and assure a first level consensual interconnectivity. Religions and spirituality always state that money is the mark of the devil, from the word mark, meaning stamp. And you cannot buy without it, as you cannot develop with it. Because money parallels your higher interconnective needs, meanings, and feelings, so you do not have to fulfill them. And since higher, interconnective needs and meanings are rewarded with love when fulfilled properly and continuously, it is exactly love that you lack continuously throughout life. And now, your life feels empty, without love. And since love is with Life and with the Divine, while money, pleasure, and selfishness are not, now everything makes sense.

The human social behavior is a form of interconnectivity, and it may be of many levels, matching the levels of behavior. Needs and feelings determine behaviors closely, and therefore needs and feelings in themselves are capable to determine living beings to interconnect harmoniously and cooperatively, at the intelligent human level. And it is through natural needs and feelings that all classes of life are formed and maintained, except for the current human society. Because money, orders, and laws parallel natural needs and natural behaviors throughout life in society, with money, orders, and laws having priority over natural needs and feelings. Or else you are accused, punished, and harassed legally, even severely.

Cognitive interconnection may be of subjective, objective, or highjective nature, depending on your point of reference. This type of cognitive interconnection should allow people to share not only feelings, ideas, impressions, and attitudes, but it should allow the sharing of thoughts and ideas, more or less directly, along with information of all kind, more or less accurately. This is what this world calls psychic abilities, including telepathy.

When you study pets and animals in general, you find them well interconnected among themselves and with their environment in general. However, humans are different than other species, since humans seem to live their life partially or entirely disabled through their highjective mind. Because humans were supposed to interconnect consciously not only with their subconscious intelligence, but also with their highconscious intelligence.

When you study very old historical records, along with mythological and religious records, you find out why, how, and who disabled humans in this manner. And those characters may still be around, still controlling this world, as crippled and as ignorant as they have made it. This is why humans may interconnect and share cognitively only feelings today, if they ever do, and they are called emphats. Or they may share information, if they can, and they are labeled with other psychic names.

Because on my classification of intelligences, I had to add an extra level for humans, the third level, just because humans cannot interconnect highconsciously even within their cognitive system, which some animal species already do. Today, science discards entirely everything related to the highjective mind and to cognitive interconnectivity, and this is why science will always remain ignorant and disabled, answering 'we don't know yet,' to every highly relevant question. And this is why science and biology state that you are always your social identity, that you are what you do for society and not who you are in life, your living nature. You are allowed to be who you are, but in your family. And this is not all, because society assigns you a consensual corporation, you live your life though that, it is a brand name, it is your name written in uppercase letters, and that is what society considers you to be, nonhuman, consensual, and nonliving. You are JOHN BROWN incorporated. Search all your forms, documents, licenses, certificates, and identity cards, to find it there, JOHN BROWN.

And this is why your environment is harsh, dry, disconnected, and dead in all scientific research, claiming that it is scientifically proven that you have to cope with the environment continuously or you go extinct, and therefore you have to work hard throughout life only to keep yourself alive in such harsh, dry, and disconnected conditions. In other words, you have to accept yourself this entire consensual austerity that you have to endure throughout life, because of what science defines to be the actual environment, which is only a dry, artificial place. And so you do, and so you live your life. And now these are the kind of news that you get on TV, while this fake, consensually imposed existence eliminates directly entire genetic lines, either carelessly or on purpose, while you accept it entirely and you even participate in it, as part of your consensually induced, disconnected behavior.

Because as a higher class of life, society was supposed to assure to you the necessary harmonious, loving, living, socially comprehensive environment for you to be able to interconnect with everybody and live your life according to your natural, intelligent human needs and feelings, at the intelligent third level, but is not the case. Your behavior should not be your continuous struggle to cope with your environment in order to fulfill your duties and needs, because at the intelligent human level, your behavior can develop the environment according to your third level developmental needs, relatively fast and even entirely, to help you interconnect and fulfill your needs. Therefore, you may end up creating and designing your own environment in a most favorable manner, but only if you are allowed to fulfill your natural needs.

What can you do? Develop yourself, since you cannot enforce others to develop if they do not want. Just develop yourself, and hope that everybody else follows. And if everybody else remains underdeveloped, then too bad for this world.

Society is the most significant part of your environment. Study your own social environment now, to find it consisting entirely of people as you. And what all want is to alter your behavior in order to match their laws and ideologies. And they do so in order to make a better, ideal world, according to their beliefs. And beliefs define thinking of the first level, while reasoning is of the third level. What people do, through all social laws, ideologies, education, and ideal expectations, they reshape your mind in an incredibly rough manner, in order for your behavior to fit the Consensual Matrix. And so what they end up doing is amputating drastically the natural part of your behavior, leaving only the consensual part. And it is exactly this consensual part of your behavior matching now the Consensual Matrix, with you integrating and maintaining it now exactly as it is, indefinitely. This harmful cognitive and behavioral procedure is highly visible within centralized regimes, yet it is present around this world, everywhere money, hierarchies, ideologies, and laws are present.

And once in this Consensual Matrix, you behave consensually through laws and regulations, paralleling the needs and feelings of life, but you can never match them. These are your social regulators now, while you use them yourself, to regulate this world in a similar manner, through similar laws and through the similar matrix. You harm yourselves in this manner and there is no way out. You can never make a better world through solutions, laws, and ideologies, no matter how often you change and adjust them, since all that you do is addressing an effect, the behavior, and not the main cause, which is this consensual, dry, disconnected matrix environment, fed to you continuously, by you.

Because this world is highly tedious to understand now with all accurate knowledge remaining hidden, yet you still have to make an effort to understand it, because there is a difference between behavior and social identity, and between what science describes as an accurate human environment and what the intelligent human environment really is. And with science and justice blaming humans themselves for their behavior, for their continuous struggle and lack of fulfillment, and with society using these same regulators to stop humans from developing themselves and this world, now you really have to study all these in order to learn what is going on in this world. Mostly since these schemes have been going on for millennia now, and it is about time to be studied and understood.

Because you do not have to keep people only underdeveloped and in a very harsh environment in order for their behavior to remain highly obedient, but you have to keep them entirely disconnected one from another and from this world, and you do so through consensual identities and consensual jurisdictions. And again, it is science implementing in society scientific laws, definitions, and models keeping people ignorant, underdeveloped, apart, and careless. And this is why when you watch the news, they give you only the number of people to have died in wars and calamities, but not their living nature, nor who they were. Because if you ever cared about all these, you never wasted a drop of food, you never ate excessively or expensive food, but only the necessary. You never fought in wars, you never gave your money to these wars, directly or indirectly, and you never ridiculed those who try to inform you of any of these.

3 YOUR CONSENSUAL BEHAVIOR IN THE CONSENSUAL MATRIX

What is the relationship between behavior, environment, identity, and interconnectivity? Simply stating, you interconnect with this world through your living nature, while using your developmental behavior in order to improve continuously your natural and social environment, bringing it gradually to the intelligent human level. And with everybody doing the same, you bring the human society to its natural, human developmental level, while developing your environment, matching your human condition. So easy to state this sentence is, yet so dense in meaning. Because it holds the key to your quest for being able to control your behavior continuously throughout life, since you cannot do so if everybody else cannot control theirs. Because this world is interconnected and it lives together, it lives through you, and it lives as you do.

What interconnection and what identity exactly? It is easier to interconnect with your family and loved ones, to form together an intelligent human environment at home in order to assure your intelligent human behavior there, since what you care the most is them, their living, intelligent identity. You see them as who they are, more than you consider them for their behavior, for what they do. Yet for the seven billion members of society, you may care less about them as individual living human beings, and you may see them through their behavior, through their needs and deeds, through their number and place in this world, through their noticeable contribution and influence upon this world and upon you. Yet everything depends on your own developmental level, because at lower developmental levels, you can eat your meals casually, while watching news from the poor countries where children starve. Because at the intelligent human level, you could not eat while seeing others starve. Some people state how they are not capable to walk by the sea because they crush the barnacles under their shoes and it feels terrible. Others state how they cannot fish anymore because they feel dreadful when they hurt the fish. These are examples of intelligent human behavior, of intelligent human feelings, and of intelligent human interconnectivity, even if this interconnectivity is made with barnacles, lobster, and fish. While all these animals interconnect to form Nature, in a living manner.

As a reference, at the zero addicted developmental level, you never care about this world, as long as you have your drugs. At the first consensual developmental level, you do exactly what you are told from above, including burning care and killing anything and anyone anywhere. At the second animal intuitive developmental level, you behave exactly as an animal, while for this world, you are considered to be exactly an animal. And if your world is of a lower developmental level, then your world considers you for what you do in this world, and for how you do so. It is no coincidence that you learn in your biology class that you are an animal. It is not a coincidence that the entire world is of a very low developmental level today.

It is not a coincidence that you are called sentient, which means feeler, because only animals follow their moods and feelings throughout their behavior while fulfilling their needs. And it is not a coincidence that society allows you to fulfill your needs up to the second animal level, taking away from you resources and accurate knowledge necessary to fulfill your intelligent human needs.

There are very high efforts in this world meant to keep you on lower developmental levels through all means, and below the human level, below the human reasoning, behavior, status, and human rights, with you agreeing to everything. Because without your human rights, you are a disabled living being, a consensual corporation, or only a wild or domestic animal, and nothing more. And since you live cognitively disconnected your entire life, you cannot know what happens, but you agree to remain below the human level. And so you call this life, and so you call this, behavior.

Try to identify a human need that humans fulfill everywhere in society and everywhere on TV among all animal behaviors that you see displayed everywhere. All movies and songs are about drugs, sex for pleasure, fights, calamities, killing, and hating. And this is how this Consensual Matrix is more as a stage, where you play your role diligently, always careful to respect all laws so you do not get in trouble. And then in your private life, you may become who you really are, the intelligent living human being, or this is the case if you are lucky enough to live your private life among highly developed people, as it is the case with many families. And don't forget to lock the door, because there is a jungle out there.

Why is the current society of the first level? It is designed to be in this manner, and even more, society is maintained at this low developmental level on purpose, through very high efforts. This is why science is ignorant today, and this is why drugs and violence are advertised continuously everywhere around, to keep you down. Because once you and this world develop, if you ever do, then you cannot be exploited anymore, and your behavior will address your true meaning in life, your human and higher meanings in life. Everything relates with the specific social niche that you create in society if you live life at a very low level, and if your behavior is of a very low level. It is more as being determined, forced, and tricked throughout life to leave your hands and feet unwashed indefinitely, only to form and maintain on your body the specific niche, habitat, or matrix necessary to grow fungus and bacteria, as in a horrible germ plantation kept on you that you carry around and maintain endlessly. Because this is the case with this entire world, and this is the Consensual Matrix.

What is your meaning in life now? The Masses are referred to as the Cattle by the Brotherhood and the Elite. This is no coincidence, and it is not even a nickname. Cattle are larger animals, and they live and work an entire lifetime for farmers unknowingly, giving them seventy, eighty, or ninety percent of their time, effort, and life. How much of your behavior do you undergo for those above you in society? Seventy percent? Ninety percent? How much can you identify your own behavior? How much money do they manage to get from you? How much do the upper social classes manage to steal from the budget of all nations? They take everything, then nations borrow more, and they take that. And this is why you go to work all day long, for them. Study this subject closely, to see you losing more than ninety percent of your time and income to those above, along with entire beloved members of your family, one after another.

It is easy to understand society by following wealth and power. Those controlling society take everything from you in every manner. Yet they do not do so directly, but only with your full agreement. You give everything away, and they take your signature, stating your agreement to give everything away, to them. Consensually, because there is no other way, you have to obey, you have to agree, or you do not get your IDs, employment, degrees, loans, certificates, titles, checks, permits, and licenses. While all these state clearly that you give everything away including your genuine, true living nature, in order to keep your consensual corporate JOHN BROWN identity. You sign for it, and you are in the matrix now, as JOHN BROWN. It is legal, by the laws of Earth, and by the higher laws everywhere else.

Can this be true? Can this entire society be a big lie? Yet how much is true and how much is false in this world today?

Let us verify now, while you decide for yourself. Science? Hundreds of thousands of distinct religions? Freedom? Righteousness? Virtues? Rights? Peace? Human behavior? Wealth? Technology? Economy? Education? History? Medicine? Great scientific achievements as the moon landing? And now, how much of what is left in this world do you assume that is still true? This entire world, how far can it actually spread? Are the stars and the Moon real, or only lights on the firmament? Why are there no pertinent real pictures of the Moon taken on its surface, but only fake, constructed images? Why is there no accurate, real picture of Earth taken from space, but only from the lower orbit and from high altitude balloons?

Make a model of what is left real in this world, to find it resembling to myths and to old religions more than to what science claims. Yet with this knowledge now, it is not hard to identify all social actors benefiting in this scheme, since they are the ones profiting out of the specific domains of society involved in this fakery. And they are the same, since they are still around, they are always around.

Even the Internet does not link computers together as many claim, but the Internet links computers to large servers. It is said that this is how it must be done, yet it is simpler to link computers together, directly, skipping servers and major computer sites censoring this world. Yet if you could link computers one to another directly, then you found freedom online, at least online. Because of interconnectivity, because free Internet can still interconnect people, if not directly through their minds, then at least through their computers. And this would still facilitate people to undergo their genuine interconnective behavior. And once interconnected, people become for each other what they truly are and not what they do, not a low, careless behavior, not a simple identification number, but the true living intelligent identity, and so this world becomes a larger family, an intelligent human society.

Even more, why do you have to go to supermarkets to buy your food? Because you do not want to grow food yourself, it would take too much time, and it would be too much of a hassle. And time is the key, because your consensual lifelong behavior takes all your time and you cannot do anything else but work and obey those controlling society, those exploiting you. And now this is how you live your life. However, you still have your inner needs nagging to live in the country, to plant a garden, and to go hunting and fishing. While the rich can even afford to pay for all these activities, since they also receive these needs, as they are human. While you still claim that you have no time and interest to live life naturally, according to your own natural needs.

It is an attitude, a social stereotype to avoid producing your own food, to eat unhealthy food, to live in big cities, to make more money, to waste more money, to take drugs, and even to go work for someone else and not for yourself. And attitudes, beliefs, and stereotypes make for the multitude of your consensual needs that you have to fulfill daily. And this comprises your consensual life, and therefore your consensual behavior.

What is your meaning in life now? It seems that about ninety percent of your meaning in life is to serve those controlling society, your masters, and you always do so with your own agreement.

You may have meanings in life of many levels, just as the needs that you fulfill daily are of various levels, since you fulfill them on behalf of all intelligences of your cognitive system, higher and lower. Therefore, your behavior may be of many types and of many levels, even simultaneously, if you know how to do so. You cannot fulfill needs and meanings in life of a level above your own developmental level, since you are not capable, you are not at that level. Chickens cannot do algebra, because they lack a cortex and a proper education. On lower developmental levels, you lack the desire, skills, abilities, and knowledge to perform anything of a higher level. As an underdeveloped human being, you still receive needs higher than your own development, because you still receive all of your natural human needs through your human nature, but you are not able to fulfill them, and so you suffer their punishment, while you remain underdeveloped. Because the natural needs that you get as a human of any developmental level are meant to develop you to the intelligent human level, they are meant to determine you to interconnect with the entire society you interconnect with your family, they are meant to determine you to help everyone as you help your loved ones at home. And because you are too underdeveloped to be able to recognize and fulfill them, these needs remain unfulfilled and they accumulate within your cognitive system, and they punish you more. This is why people have to take drugs and seek entertainment and random social interaction, in order to make up for the rewards that they miss by not fulfilling needs that are higher than their own development.

Sometimes, you are not even capable to identify your very high natural needs and meanings in life, you fail fulfilling them, and therefore you are punished severely, with boredom and depression. This is exactly what depression and bipolar are, and medicine cures them with more drugs, powerful drugs that cut through you brain, so next time there are no higher intelligences left to send you higher needs. And now, by living your life within a first level world that advertises drugs continuously and that considers you to be an animal, an addict, or a servant of the hierarchy, good luck with your natural higher needs, because you will never be able to fulfill these, while you will join the rest of the crowd to ridicule those who still try to fulfill theirs.

And this is why you see an entire world drugged and medicated, Masses and Brotherhood alike, because people cannot fulfill their needs throughout life, and they cannot keep their inner harmony. And then their inner punishment becomes too harsh, the happiness is absent, they take drugs to compensate, and the drugs lobotomize them, they amputate their cognitive system. And in this manner, they do not receive needs and punishment anymore, yet they still feel terrible and empty, when sober. And so they disconnect from the wider world entirely, to remain enclosed in the consensual world.

Today, education and medicine identify highly developed children of the Masses to label them with autism just because they stand apart from the crowd, and the prescribed drugs that they have to take destroy their cognitive system from the start, from childhood. They receive no higher needs anymore, they have no higher meaning in life anymore, and this is how they live their life.

Because these children are the ones breaking through the consensual social environment, now and when they grow up, while society is meant to be and remain at the first developmental level, indefinitely. Otherwise, this global, exploiting enterprise cannot work. And therefore, all individuals must be of the first developmental level, in order for everything to work properly. Otherwise, you might want to be free, to live your own life, to do what you were supposed to do naturally, to love and to be happy, in a living, natural world where you fit in, among your loved ones and among the rest of this world, but you cannot have all these, not in a first level consensual society.

Just look around. You see streets, buildings, cars, and people passing by, and nothing else. What else should it be there? People living normal lives together. Do people live normal lives anymore? People should live everywhere, together, mostly outside buildings, since individual habitats disconnect people. Where are the common living places? Where can people be and live together? In bars? There are parks, yet parks are there for you to be in nature, but not to be in nature along with the rest of this world. If you try to live and sleep anywhere in these so-called common places, on streets and in parks, because there is nothing else, you break the law and you get in trouble. You also break the law if you live together with everybody else, which is a significant part of your natural human behavior. You break the law if you interconnect with everybody else. Therefore, you break the law if you are genuinely human. And this is the Consensual Matrix that everyone should address, not you.

The first level meaning in life is consensual, and it is to

serve those above you unconditionally. Your meaning of the second level relates to all animals, and it comprises all needs meant to keep you alive, as physiological needs, along with security and recovery needs. These are animal needs, and humans share them, along with all intelligences from the wider world. Intelligent human societies should assure the fulfillment of these needs to everybody, by default, allowing everybody to tend undisturbed to their human and higher needs. However, society makes it hard for you to be able to fulfill even these animal needs throughout life, because you lack time or money, or because you have to obey moral laws, or because you are ridiculed and marginalized. And this is how you remain stuck on lower level needs, and you cannot develop. Or you have to sell yourself into servitude and this is how you remain on the first developmental level, as it is the case with the Masses and with the Brotherhood.

And then, when you manage to understand any of these, and when you aspire for your human development, society advertises drugs directly, implicitly, and subliminally, in order to encourage their use, and you give in, starting with a beer a day. And so your development is over, from one single beer, from one single coffee, and from one single soft drink, because what these do to your cognitive system is never what you aspire. You lose your necessary high desire and high developmental abilities, and you give in and obey. Or society feeds drugs directly to you through food, drinks, water, air, and medication, and this is how you decay to the zero addicted level, even indefinitely.

How many genuinely developed humans are in this world today? It is hard to tell, but these cannot be in the Brotherhood or in the Elite, since these are the consensual social classes making and keeping this world underdeveloped exactly as it is. While any intelligent human being from among the upper social classes would do everything in order to save the people of Earth from themselves, and then they would use their entire wealth and influence to instate an intelligent human society. Is this the case?

It is rumored that humanity is enslaved from higher above, by higher beings or by powerful nonhuman civilizations, while those controlling society today compromise and obey, which may or may not be true, as everything else. While there is an entire Consensual Matrix formed of most of intelligent living beings, civilizations, and intelligences of the wider world, enslaving humanity just as well.

What is the difference between a world with the Consensual Matrix present, and one without it? It is exactly the difference between Life and death, consensual death, and you can feel it. Because in a genuine living world, you do everything that you feel, want, think, and find necessary, since you are free to do as you feel and please. While in the Consensual Matrix, there are always consensual constraints, deliberate shortages, and lack of cooperation even from your loved ones, if you have any loved ones in a consensual world, since these are called otherwise. Even your Certificate of Marriage is in the name of your brands or corporations, since these get married. Try to change that to lowercase letters, and you cannot.

And the consensual is everywhere. How many movies do you see where people actually study on their own, the entire movie? None. There are some movies with geniuses and with very capable people, but these are capable by default, they are already gifted, they are very lucky to be in this manner the entire movie, and they never have to study. While they still display a lower level behavior as anyone that you see on TV. Because TV advertises ignorance and idiocy, along with an entire lower level lifestyle.

Then how can you develop throughout life? How can you undergo an intelligent human behavior throughout life? First through knowledge, but knowledge is fake and even harmful today. All pertinent knowledge is not only absent from TV, but it is also absent from bookstores and even from the Internet, and consequently, this world dumbs down and decays. Art is fake ever since the Impressionism and it cannot address your highconscious anymore. And it is the same with everything that may be considered human achievement in this world, it is faked and dumbed down. Medicine is fake and even fatal. Education is fake, indoctrinating and time consuming. Science is dogma, economy wastes people's time and resources while it trashes the environment. The moon landing is faked, and probably everything that it is said to exist beyond the low orbit of Earth is not real either. While true scientists are kept out of job, and if they ever engage in independent research, then their reports are ignored, and their books are censored.

Absence of intelligent human behavior and achievements in this world implies the fact that this is not an intelligent human society, this is not an intelligent human civilization, and therefore no one can obtain a human status in the wider world. Without an intelligent human status, people of Earth may be owned and exploited as cattle by anyone who is in this business, and this has always been the case on Earth. And now you understand your behavior, you understand why it has to be consensual, you understand why the laws of society interfere with your natural human behavior, and you understand that your actual, instinctual behavior is not actually bad or savage, but it is normal, natural, and probably even genuinely human.

But are you always genuinely human? You are, at least at this moment, just because you feel your higher needs and you fulfill them, since you take the time to study intelligent human knowledge. Yet if you have to spend all your time at work, you may be too tired to invest in developing yourself. Besides, your mind and reasoning have to be in their best shape in order to undergo and assure an intelligent human behavior. If you drink something, smoke something, or if you are bombarded with sex advertisement continuously, then you certainly remain on lower developmental levels, just because all needs coming to you are of lower, animal level. And then, if you happen to be from the current consensual, hierarchic Brotherhood, you have to serve those above. And when they tell you what books to read and how to develop, you have to obey and do just that, so you still lack the necessary freedom that genuinely developed humans have, in order to undergo their human behavior and fulfill their human and higher meanings in life.

As a reference, genuinely developed humans seek continuous development, along with genuine art, righteousness, truth, intelligent human company, along with all the necessary means to reach out and help this world in every manner, either through true teaching, eradication of hunger and sickness in this world, researching accurate, useful technologies, and helping anyone in need. Look around, to see the true capable teachers of this world losing their jobs and being kicked out of education. It is the same with the true, capable scientists, since they lose their jobs in every manner, because they tend to ignore the scientific references fed to them to consider and follow in their research, being dogmatic, fake, irrelevant, and many times harmful to this world. And when true doctors persist to help and cure various people, they are accused of malpractice, harassment, and of working without a license, and they are prosecuted. While those who avoid common drugs while aspiring to develop in any manner are ridiculed in every way, marginalized, and harassed.

What can you do? Nothing, there is no hope. And everything relates with behavior, because once you start displaying intelligent human behavior, you are avoided indefinitely, you are ridiculed and punished, you lose your job and your family, you lack opportunities of any kind, you lack a place in society, and you become absent and invisible in this world. You are already dead in this manner, because in this world, what you do is the only thing that matters. There are people losing their online accounts for posting true knowledge and pertinent information. Genuine teachers get phone calls at school from officials incriminating them implicitly or directly, while many others lose their families in a similar manner, being incriminated methodically until their spouses divorce them and they take the children with them when they leave. You lose your friends in this manner just because they get phone calls from specific authorities seeking information regarding most dreadful circumstances concerning you, and so your friends and neighbors stop talking with you, they keep their children far away from you, and this kind of examples are many to give.

So, why do you behave as you do? Because there is no other way, your environment offers you one lifestyle, one behavior, and so you take it and live your life in this manner, as everyone does. Why are there no other possibilities? Everyone does the same, with those seeking a behavior matching their human needs compromised and removed from society.

Yet if your behavior is consensual, harmful, and exploitive, then why can't you notice it? Why is it not obvious to you? Because it has always been in this manner, and you are used to it. In contrast, your natural needs seem strange many times, and they seem in dissonance with what is demanded from you in society. But you consider them to be your cognitive malfunctions, your bad attitude, your fault, probably because you are incapable throughout life, or this is what you assume. You fail in society continuously, and it seems that you are never as good as others.

Reasons for your persistent unidentifiable higher level needs are many. You assume that you fail to entertain yourself, or you fail to watch the best movies. And so you take some more drugs or you go out to see some friends that you have never cared about and who seem to hate you anyway, tomorrow is another day of work, and this is how you live your life, on a very low level, when you are more developed. Or this is the case if you are not held at work continuously, which is the case in many nations.

Boredom is not a lower level need, but it is an intelligent human need. It is the need for learning and developing and not the need for entertainment. What happens is that living beings have to eat continuously, because they need materials and energy. The human intelligences are cognitive in nature, and therefore similarly to food, they need cognitive substance to subsist, cognitive food coming in the form of knowledge, which has to be important and accurate. Your intelligences seek knowledge from you along with help with the development of various cognitive abilities. And you must fulfill these needs, many times continuously throughout the day and throughout life. And the more capable you are, the more you have to study and exercise your mind throughout life, otherwise it decays and you lose it. And if you ever take drugs or poisonous additives, then you really lose it and it feels terrible. If you fail to provide the exact knowledge that your intelligences demand in the exact amount that they need and exactly when they need it, your intelligences starve, they decay, they shrink, they lose power, they lose consistency and abilities, they are amputated, and you lose them. And since you use your mind in order to assess and understand your own mind, now being cognitively disabled, you do not even have the chance to know that your intelligences are gone or that they have ever been with you in the first place.

Even when you are forced to behave on lower developmental levels, you are still human, and therefore you still receive human needs, along with higher level needs, as long as you are not already cognitively disabled. You have the mind but you lack its power, knowledge, or development, since all are of a lower developmental level. You mistakenly identify some of these higher level needs as common lower level needs, you fulfill them that way through a lower behavior, it does not really match, and surprisingly for you, you are punished instead of being rewarded. As it happens with the needs for higher development and higher social behavior, which you mistakenly try to fulfill through watching random TV or through meeting and chatting with random people. While you were supposed to engage in art or in a specific research that you seemed to have been interested at one time or another in the past, and you were supposed to make friends interested in these specific topics.

As an intelligent human being, your cognitive system does not send you randomly some hunger now and some thirst later, with needs to play tennis two times a week, and then you have your needs for a coffee every hour or so, when you also like to watch the news. All these may seem to you to be human needs since they may seem to define humans the most, since humans seem to do all these and more. Because as a genuinely developed human being, you fulfill all your lower level needs by default as fast as you can, including your physiological needs, to have time for your human and higher level needs, because these are more fulfilling, and you want them to take all your time.

Why would you ever waste your time with higher level behavior? Why suffering and enduring so hard throughout an entire life? Are your virtue and your sense of duty for this world so developed, that you are ready now to give up your entire life for world beautification and for the protection of wild whales? Well, no. Because at the higher developmental level, living an entire life involved in addiction and animal needs seems so low and is so dreadful to accept and undergo, that you are ready to do everything to engage in a genuinely higher behavior in order to match your own reasoning and capabilities. Because your higher intelligences punish you so hard when you waste your life while you are highly developed, that you give in. And then, when you manage to fulfill your higher level needs exactly as you should, then the happiness, satisfaction, and completion that you receive are so extraordinarily rewarding, that no feeling that anyone receives on any lower developmental level compares. It is never a matter of choice, of what you could do today to pass some time away, to feel good, or to make others feel good, but it is a matter of how to match your highest abilities and expectations with the highest demanding world circumstance there is. You find in this manner your most accurate niche in society, as high in level as your own developmental level can offer. And since these are not available because all social niches are low in level, or they are hidden or forbidden, you seek some more, and eventually you find a way, you find your own place in this world, as high in level as you desire, just because this world is relatively diverse, not too bad and not too scarce in opportunities. And then, higher beings get involved sometimes to work at your side and it is beautiful, therefore, higher behaviors are not that tedious at all, and you never really want to live your life on lower developmental levels instead.

To give an example, it is as when you are in high school and you find it too tedious and too boring, and you just wish hard to be back in the first grade and do all that instead. Because it would be easier and therefore more pleasant and more fulfilling. Or this is what you assume. But what if it really happens, and somehow, now you are privileged to attend the first grade elementary school, instead of college or high school. And you are thrilled, because they will still give you your degrees. Yet how pleasant and entertaining first grade really is, and it should make for a very amusing life. Right? No, not at all. It might be amusing the first hour or the first day, enjoying being able to relax while displaying your extraordinary knowledge, and while earning extraordinary school results. But having to sit down all day long doing all those childish activities, numbers, songs, and gluing paper, day after day, it is not fun anymore. Since this is why nobody goes back to the first grade of school, regardless of how easy it is.

Yet in the current society it is different, because the current society is at the elementary level in everything concerning human development and human knowledge. Because in the current consensual human society, you have to remain in the first grade for life, or you get in trouble, and it is terrible when you get in trouble. By the end of the month, you are a wreck, and you have to drink heavily at home in order to cope with yourself, because all that stupid activity drives you insane. Teachers are fine at school, because teachers work hard to manage the class and teach everything, they are already performing at their third developmental level, so lucky them. But you are already mad, after only the first semester back in the first grade. You are already addicted to vodka now, you snap and you show your bad behavior, you are already the worst kid in class while you are an adult, you cannot control yourself, you are a menace, the teacher sends you to a psychologist, you get labeled with alphabet sicknesses, you take medication and it feels dreadful, while life is never the same. But in only one year, your mind is amputated, to resemble in capabilities to the mind of a little kid, a very severely mentally sick little kid. And so you have to finish your first grade now as a mentally disabled child, but you are capable to sit down in your little corner for hours in a row, and you are even capable to look at the teacher absently the entire day. Which is an achievement. So yes, now you are capable to pay attention, and to learn. Not that anything makes much sense anymore.

And if you do not believe it, just try to take the medication yourself, and you become a vegetable, while you are always in terrible pain, discomfort, and depression. And so you get to remain in the first grade indefinitely, as a student with mental disabilities, and you get to have your own teachers, counselors, psychologists, and teaching assistants.

There is more to this example. There are rumors that there are calls made up there for help, to save this world because it is considered below expectations up there. And a large number of highly developed intelligences come now to be able to do something about this world, use their extraordinary capabilities to find a solution and stop the social control and the social exploitation, stop the sickness, addictions, and cognitive decay, or at least for them to be among people randomly, teach them, inspire them, be with them, and therefore help them change their behavior.

But all higher beings coming here in very large numbers to help are already accounted for, as they are diagnosed with Autism in early childhood, and end up needing help just as well. And we are back where we started, because behavior is an effect, not a main cause, and therefore with this strategy, they lose their time and effort by coming here in this first grade school world.

But it seems to happen with them now exactly what happened in our example. Because most of these superhero higher beings are mad by now, heavily addicted, medicated, and labeled with mental illnesses and with behavioral dysfunctions. Or if they have made it so far, they find themselves in the current hierarchic Brotherhood now, instating, implementing, and maintaining this harmful Consensual Matrix causing problems the entire time. And so this profitable social enterprise continues now, harvesting on highly developed higher beings.

This is exactly how life is, because regardless of your age, you still have to take drugs and to be entertained continuously in this first grade life. This is exactly what all intelligences do in this world because it is too low in development, and it probably ends up harming intelligences more than helping them in any way.

Why do all these happen? Why exactly do you run insane? You do not only run insane, but you are supposed to die under these circumstances. Because your intelligences do not allow you to occupy an invalid, improper environment, considerably lower than what you should, since it is not adequate for you to fulfill their needs for knowledge. Intelligences seek accurate information throughout life, depending on what they need, and you have to find and give them exactly that information, at that exact complexity level. You either find it directly in books or you have to undergo specific experiences, and this is why you have to engage in all activities throughout life. This is how you may end up going around this world or taking a vacation on a cruise ship, or you go to live in New Zealand for a year. You seek and try everything, you do everything that your intelligences demand, you consider your various experiences to be delicacies in life while they feed your intelligences well, and so you are fine. Because if you cannot do all these, and you can never do so by attending first grade classes indefinitely, then your intelligences will force you in every manner to obey. And if you still fail to identify your higher level needs and fulfill them, then Life kills you, with mental sicknesses and with free radicals.

Is it hard to believe? Just go sit in a corner for a day or so in a quiet room with no windows, stare at a wall the entire time, to see how your higher intelligences react. Try it for five minutes or so, to study the boredom, anxiety, discomfort, depression, sadness, and lack of fulfillment in life. Try not to starve your intelligences too much, but make sure that you memorize the feeling, because that is exactly how the need for higher learning and higher development feels like. Make sure that you do not mistake it with the need for drugs or entertainment, because these are of the zero level. Because if you already take drugs even occasionally, which is what everyone does, then you cannot feel your need for higher development anymore, but you feel your need to drink another beer or to smoke another smoke, and that is exactly what you do instead.

As a reference, drugs start with caffeine, aspartame, and MSG, going up to the most powerful drugs. Today, opioids and cannabinoids are in fashion, and if your family doctor prescribes them, then you do not even have to pay for them. If you take these, your development drops in level, until you become addicted. And if you keep on increasing the dose, your behavior becomes so out of control, that you can understand this entire book from your own experience. Yet once you are addicted, there might be no way out. Unless you pay that pleasure back, with severe pain and with depression.

And now, if you do not take drugs, is it still tedious to engage in these third level activities? As a genuine living human being, are you forced to perform tedious activities as performing research in advanced physics or travelling around this world? No, because as an intelligent human being, you do what you need, more than you do what you want or must. As an intelligent human being, you need to engage in genuine science or genuine art, among other human activities, and no one forces you, not even you. And if you happen not to receive higher human needs, then you may do as you please. You may fulfill needs of any level in life, since society seems to offer their fulfillment, except for the human needs. Your highconscious wants you immersed entirely in human activities, in human behavior, with piano lessons and research in true physics and true psychology, being around good friends that are well acquainted in these disciplines and therefore seek similar continuous studies throughout life, and you engage in this study and in this work only to be able to help this world as much as you can, with a new type of nonpolluting engine, or with a new, better method of storing electric energy in car accumulators. And you can really spend your entire time in this type of human environment, regardless if you are more or less intelligent. Yet if you mention all these in society today, you are ridiculed, and then you are avoided.

And this is exactly why life seems dry and meaningless today, because there is no meaning in life when you live it below your capabilities, below your achievements, and below your expectations. And now, with everyone lacking exactly this type of feelings and this type of fulfillment, people have to live life drugged and continuously entertained and medicated, only to be able to compensate for their expected human satisfaction, human behavior, and human environment. This is exactly the problem with this world, since everybody is forced to live the life of an addict or of an animal, while carrying the innate cognitive powers and abilities of a highly capable intelligent human being. Because everybody is in the first grade at school today, regardless of their age, and it certainly hurts without drugs, entertainment, medicine, and ideologies.

And this should be already obvious and no one should ever have to make it clear, that once you are equipped with an extraordinary brain, which is the most powerful cognitive system in the known universe, you cannot live the lifestyle of an arthropod, or you feel so terribly bored and worthless if you do, that you cannot control yourself anymore and you run insane. Yet this is exactly what you are today, human, this is exactly how you live your life today, below the human level, and now this happens to you, you feel bored and down many times, your achievements in life seem below your expectations, you drink probably too much sometimes, you get into arguments and into inadequate circumstances and you lose control, you destroy your life and nothing is the same anymore, the medication that you take does not work anymore, you take harder and harder drugs, you lose your good friends and you keep the worst, and you are already past the point of no return, and there is not much to do about it. While arthropods might have a better life. Probably because their brain, if they have one, matches their behavior, meaning, and fulfillment. Because yours seems to have been too capable.

And this happens with everyone, as you are using the most powerful cognitive system in the universe to watch TV, drink beer, and go to work all day long where you tie a nut in an assembly line, nut after nut, or where you flip burgers and butter buns, all day long. And so you become more and more depressed, until life becomes out of control and you snap, with everyone still wondering why. Because when you have a powerful human brain you have to use it continuously at its high capacity and through all its high abilities only to keep it in shape, or you lose it and you cannot control your behavior anymore.

Yet this is not the only problem. What happens is that your brain is a living cognitive system and not a mechanism or a muscle tissue to flex it daily and have it in shape and good to go. Your brain does not seek only continuous learning and continuous cognitive training, but your mind seeks wellness and righteousness in this world, and it is ready to send you the necessary needs and feelings in order to make you become involved in making this world a better place. If you ignore or temper with this type of higher needs and higher meanings in any manner, you lose your brain, you become very depressed, you fall ill, you cannot control yourself, and you have to be medicated, drugged, intoxicated, and out of the way you go. Since Life will bring someone else in this world to replace you, if you remain incapable to fulfill your higher level human needs as you should, to fulfill her.

Why exactly having to change this world? Why making it a better place? Because the human mind seeks a human behavior and a human environment both, probably just because a human environment assures a human behavior, but more likely, because a human environment assures a living human nature. Or more precisely, a human environment assures that you are who you are in life, that you are the unique living being, more than your own behavior and social specialization, which are what you do in this world. And this is the case probably because your genuine, intelligent, living human nature relates more to your mind, to your intelligence, and to your inner self, more than it relates to your behavior.

Why having a human nature and why having a human environment? What exactly is so important with these? Because we can already feel our needs and feelings seeking and referring continuously to a human environment and to a human nature. Identity, behavior, and environment seem to be highly related, and they tend to show up in all my research together. You must always be able to integrate perfectly in your environment in order to assure harmony and interconnectivity, and you certainly do so through your intelligences, since they send you the needs that determine your behavior.

But why exactly having to match your environment? Why having to match your true nature or identity through your behavior? And why are these three interconnected? Because your entire human behavior might not be the last element on your lifeline of causality, the final effect, but the entire human behavior may have an effect, a meaning, which is to create a proper human environment. If this is the case, then the entire lifeline of causality is cyclical in nature. The environment facilitates the fulfillment of your needs through your thinking, all resulting in your behavior. While your behavior is meant to modify and construct a proper human environment, which is capable to allow the fulfillment of higher level needs through your human thinking, resulting in your human behavior that is meant to develop the environment. Your lifeline of causality seems cyclical and repetitive, yet it manifests a continuous improvement and therefore a continuous development. While development is a main meaning in life, and a very important higher level human need.

I refer to this entire activity taking place throughout your lifeline of causality as being your causal behavior. Your causal behavior is cyclic when it is developmental, it is persistent and perseverant in nature, and it stands at the base of your continuous process of cognitive development when it is allowed to manifest freely. This cyclic, developing causal behavior, when it is cognitive in nature, stands at the base of the intuitive thinking, and I model it in all the books of this series related to reasoning and intelligence. You should certainly identify and facilitate this cyclical, developing behavior throughout life, as you should do with the rest of your needs and behaviors.

It is relevant to state here that the cyclical developing behavior does not result only in the improvement of your environment and behavior, but it develops all elements of your lifeline of causality. It happens that humans are capable to modify easily their environment, and this is what they might improve the most, because other species are less capable to change their environment. And this is how they end up improving any other element on their lifeline of causality. They end up improving themselves and their behavior as much as they can, and so we find them highly perceptive and responsive to the environment. Animals will even change their physical appearance and bodily characteristics in time, only to match eventual natural and social changes in their environment.

4 YOUR BEHAVIOR, NATURE, AND IDENTITY IN A COMPREHENSIVE ENVIRONMENT

We have noticed another important result, that the same cyclical causality takes place within your human nature. Your behavior, your identity, and your environment are placed on a cyclical lifeline of causality determining each other repeatedly. Therefore, all facets of who you are relate to each other, as they are facets of a same main identity, you. You are the objective body along with its behavior in this world. You are the intelligence with its needs and reasoning, and you are the living being. Life, intelligence, and physical body define you simultaneously as a oneness, as one, they are interconnective as one, and therefore you are one, or you are a oneness. The word 'one' defines you as existing, being alive, and being intelligent, since you can never be one without another, you are one. You are also a oneness of all intelligences of your cognitive system, and of all your cells and cellular components. And there are zillions of these within you, with you being only one of them. While you are one, you are oneness. And this is an extraordinary achievement.

Take your reference to the highest level now, to consider

the same for the entire wider world to define the One. The One is Life, Intelligence, along with everything that exists everywhere, ever, interconnected. The facets of the One are Life, Intelligence, the universe, the interconnectivity, and the Divine, all being the One. And this is why religions and spirituality venerate the One through one of its perspective, Interconnectivity. This is why some venerate Life or the Divine Mother, Mother Earth, or Mother Mary. Others venerate the One as the Supreme Intelligence, as the Supreme Being, and as the Universal Mind. And now, more recently, science venerates the One as the universe, through all its dogma, beliefs, and scientific references, forcing the entire world to do the same.

We have considered only normal, natural circumstances so far, because people's behavior is forced, consensual, and controlled, and this is why it determines and it constructs a consensual, inadequate, lower level environment, meant to compromise your achievements, and consequently, meant to keep the entire world helpless and underdeveloped. And this is not the only problem, because with your human and higher needs impossible to fulfill without an intelligent human environment, you receive no pleasure at all from life, you have no fulfillment, no meaning, no place, and no acceptance. And this is why you have to do what everybody does, you engage excessively in drugs, entertainment, and in animal needs, any animal need rewarding you well with excessive pleasure, as sexual activities, eating excessively, and engaging in reckless social competition. And this is how you live your life.

Therefore, if you ever want to change your behavior, you must be able to control your environment. You have to choose it, design it, alter it in every manner when necessary, but make it as it is supposed to be for you, since you are human. Make it a human environment. And this is possible, since today, the informational technology is relatively advanced and it allows you to live your life in the environment that you desire, even in the human environment, online. Or you may do so at first, because once sufficient people achieve their intelligent human developmental level, together, people can change their entire environment accordingly. And the environment is the key.

What exactly is the environment? You might assume that environment means green trees, rocks, clean air, nature in general, and bad weather, since this is what science promotes, but there is more. People alter the environment as they please and mostly as they need, while animals cope with the environment and they adapt their behavior and even their bodily appearance to cope with the environment, in order to be able to fulfill their needs. Look around, to see that nothing is left of the original environment after your city was built. Everything is changed, and now it fits perfectly your lifestyle and your behavior. Yet this is only the built environment, and not at all the human environment.

The environment is formed of all environmental elements or environmental details, and these are everything that exists. Among these, the specific environmental conditions influencing you directly or implicitly form your own environment. Your own environment may be favorable and unfavorable, through its favorable and unfavorable elements, and you know them very well. These may be physical, cognitive, social, higher, consensual, natural, and familial. We focus here on your conditional environment, since this addresses you either favorably or unfavorably.

As you notice, your environment is more than your habitat, since your environment can be more than natural and physical. Your habitat is the place or area where you live, which may be your city, community, or house. Your environment is your habitat, plus your food, water, books, music, transportation, clothes, mates, Internet, and family, since your environment is the summation of all places, materials, resources, and information that you need in order to fulfill all your needs and meaning in life. Your environment is the first element on your lifeline of causality, causing, determining, or allowing everything else to happen, determining in this manner your behavior.

I divide the environment into domains. You have your natural or physical environment, which is material and objective in nature, as the roof over your head and the food that you eat. Your social environment is what you interact with the most throughout life, and it consists of people as you, along with their influence upon you and upon this world. If you divorce society to go live in solitude somewhere in the country for the rest of your life, you may see how you never escape your social environment, because it follows you everywhere, in every manner. While you do not even change your lifestyle when you relocate, let alone your behavior.

Next, you have your subjective environment, comprising your thoughts and daydreams, along with your online environment, since these are subjective in nature, not material and objective. Other environmental domains are ideal, abstract, cognitive, and consensual.

Your consensual environment is abstract, and it consists of all legal details of your life, as all licenses, permits, signatures, degrees, laws, jurisdictions, and hierarchies. It seems that this is only a simple accumulation of necessary documents that you have to tend to throughout life, yet your consensual environment is vast, pertinent, and accurate enough to form an entire abstract reality acting as a standalone reality apart from the One, since the One is alive, natural, and real, it is Life. And in this entire consensual environment, you have your own consensual self, which is your brand or consensual corporation, which is your name written in uppercase letters. And regardless if you know it or not, throughout most of your life, you are constrained to behave consensually not as a living human being, since you cannot do so, but as a consensual self, which is your name written in uppercase letters. And if you are from the Brotherhood, you know it in various degrees, depending on your status. While if you are from the Masses, you are made to believe that your name written in uppercase letters in your identity. Study all your documents, to find your consensual corporation mentioned on all of them, just because these are its own documents and not yours. Everything is its existence, and not at all your life as you are made to believe. And this is the difference between the current consensual society and the intelligent human society, because the intelligent human society is an overall human family, it is not the Consensual Matrix, and you do not need documents in order to be anywhere in the human society, just as you do not need documents at home in your family, because you are a natural living human being.

Yet there is more to consider, since the intelligent human society is not exactly erased and replaced by the Consensual Matrix and now you have to fight it back in order to gain your human rights, since this is only a stereotype that you pick up from the media and entertainment. But the intelligent human society is always present, as long as there are living human beings around, only that it remains ignored through ignorance or oath. This is how you can still travel everywhere without documents and even without a passport, and this is hidden from everybody. This is how the police cannot interfere with you as a living human being, along with the entire juridical system.

This means that, currently, you behave either as a consensual corporation, or as a living human being. And if you are from the Masses, you never distinguish between the two, since the media and entertainment never do. While if you are from the Brotherhood, you know all these, in various degrees. Yet since you live your life under oath in the Brotherhood, you have to behave as a consensual corporation around the clock.

As stated, you can break down environments into elements. All environmental elements may affect you or they remain neutral to you. The specific environmental elements affecting you are called conditions, and these may be favorable and unfavorable, and together they form the human condition in life and in this world. The specific favorable environmental conditions are called niches.

For example, rabbits have a different niche than fish, pine trees, and roaches, and this is why these species can live together even within the same habitat, without interfering with each other. You may assume that all species should be able to live endlessly on Earth, just because their niches never interact, yet this is not true. Besides, many species occupying a same niche enter in competition throughout time, with the weakest to depart the Earth environment, and this is why there are only a few species for each niche today.

The deer niche is easier to define: grass, water, air, security, mates, and lack of predators. The human niche includes food and security, along with mates and proper temperature, and lately it includes Internet and fast transportation, medicine, education and minimum income guaranteed. Notice how today, the niches of all species of Earth interconnect and integrate together to cover the entire habitat of Earth, leaving not a single gap unoccupied. Because any available gap in the environment becomes a new niche for a new species, or for the first existing species to adapt to this newly available niche or niche element.

We notice the obvious change in the Earth environment that humans have brought along through their entire behavior. Humans trash this world and warm it up or this is what science claims, yet all change in the Earth environment may not necessarily come from a bad or irresponsible human behavior, but from a natural, expected one. Species went extinct on Earth in large numbers ever since humanity took over the globe, yet it happened because humans took over their niche in every manner, not because humans killed these animals directly. Humans could not take over other niches directly, but they only took over adjacent individual niche elements. And now, with one niche element missing from their niche, those species had to vacate the entire niche, took over other niches themselves, or they adapted in any manner to do without the missing niche element.

Not all niches are compatible from one species to another. Humans cannot eat grass. But since the human habitat takes a large space, it expanded, and it took over the habitat of grass. Herbivores have grass in their own niche, and without it, they dropped in number until they went extinct. Yet humans reproduced and replaced all lost herbivores, still making for a similar number of individual living beings throughout the ecosystem. This world is not actually dying, but only changing, which it always does. And since humans are more developed in all levels, this world itself has ascended in development, along with Life herself here in this world. This happened in a more complex manner, since humans limited the habitat of all herbivores, and now all herbivores had to compete for the remaining free grassy habitat. The weakest ones went extinct, the carnivores and the rest of the species above them on their food chain entered a stronger competition, and the weakest of them went extinct.

Yet this is the case with all highly successful species and not only with humans, since they tend to multiply excessively and therefore to outgrow and expand their niche, habitat, and environment, to cover this world. As grass itself did, not too long time ago, because it expanded rapidly to span the globe, forcing to extinction a multitude of smaller ground plant species. Yet you could not even have fertile land without grass, because the wind erodes the fertile land everywhere there is no grass. Flies, mosquitoes, spiders and ants took over this world in the same manner, along with dogs, cats, and horses.

And the same happens throughout the social environment, where society itself took over the human environment in a very similar manner. And now, you cannot live outside society at all, and so you have to use money and Google, for life. Even more, capitalism is the only social ideology today, you have to obey it well, and this is how you have to use money for life, money that belongs directly to the Upper Brotherhood.

And once you use money, you are the one giving to the rich all your wealth, work, values, and achievements throughout your life. Technically you work and live for them, you hand to them your own lifelong behavior, over ninety-nine percent of it. And there is nothing that you can do, because your natural niche is not available anymore, so you cannot live there in a natural manner anymore. Now only your social consensual niche is open, you were born in it anyway, and now you have to be there.

When you lack awareness of the exploitation done on you,

you are considered to be cattle, since you are made use of, harvested, and exploited continuously throughout life, without your knowledge. You are even sold on the stock exchange market, and there are ways for you to enter your own social identification number or your own corporation number in order to see your current stock value. Or this is the case if you are a public entity, because if you are owned in private, then you belong to a private owner. Yet they never consider you the living human being but only your corporation. And this is how they never exploit you the living human being, but only your corporation. And this happens with everybody from the Masses and the Brotherhood, since all members of these two social classes are owned in every manner, but only their corporation, or their names in uppercase letters.

Yet as you notice, you can never have corporations walking around without you the living human being. These corporations are you, since you go to work and everywhere else. Yet if the Consensual Matrix considers you a corporation, you cannot do anything about it. Even more, you are obliged by law to obtain a Certificate of Birth for all your children, and this is how you brand them, making them into corporations and part of the Consensual Matrix. Yet it is not you the living being obliged to brand your children, but your corporation, while you do not brand your children, but only their corporations, once you instate them, yet what is the difference?

And what exactly can you do about it? Because if this is the consensual agreement among all the people, this is how everybody behaves today, by agreement, or consensually, since this is what agreement means. While if you remain ignorant of this entire agreement, with you always in it and expected the entire time to know it well, which is the case with the Masses, then this is exactly how the Masses are exploited. And this is how this entire legal procedure remains disguised. And when you are demanded to enhance it continuously when you are from the Brotherhood, while burning your care throughout rituals and while having a big laugh of this entire enforced circumstance since you profit the entire time while keeping it enforced, this is the disguised part.

Many times, people are owned by people who are owned by people who are owned by entire families who are owned by higher families, all the way up to the Elite, who owns this world. The multi-billionaires that you see in the news are owned several times over by more powerful people and families, that may be hidden or in the open.

To be more precise, people do not own people since it is not allowed by the laws of Earth and by the higher laws of the wider world, but people own that consensual corporation of other people, the JOHN BROWN branded or incorporated name, which is a genuine corporation, and therefore it can be exploited, bought, and sold in every manner. Yet with you being forced to live your life through this corporation, which is considered to be the consensual you. Within the Higher Brotherhood, not only that people are owned as corporation, but their Families are owned in this manner, as brand names, with most of them to be highly valuable. Families own families who own families who own entire batches of people, down to the last chicken in the market.

And as seen, there is one difference between those in the Masses and those in the Brotherhood, the fact that those in the Brotherhood are aware of the current social scheme. Yet even when the Masses become aware, they are never considered Brothers, but they are ignored and exploited just as well. Technically, people in the Brotherhood are not cattle, since they are aware of their status and meaning in this world, that they are owned and exploited for profit entirely by those on the social layers above. And people who are owned knowingly and willingly are called slaves. Slaves know that they are property, but cattle do not, while they are exploited relatively similarly.

To be more precise, cows are still aware of their lack of freedom yet they do not want to escape, or cannot escape. Even more, cows cannot communicate in order to state clearly that they do not wish to be exploited, in case that they do not wish to be exploited. It is the same with the people from the

Masses, since their ignorance is considered as a tacit agreement to be exploited, to be cattle. Even more, all signatures that you place near your name written in uppercase letters is an agreement that you may be owned, since your entire ownership is always associated with your name being written in uppercase letters, because it represents a separate self, a corporation, many times not even being associated with you the living human being. And you have to have this separate identity in order to be owned, just because you have your human rights from birth, and cannot be owned as a living being. And through your human rights, no other human may ever own or exploit you in any manner, and this includes exploiting you as a livestock, slave, and even worker.

Note how 'cattle' and 'slave' are not nicknames but genuine statuses and definitions, and they are even accepted by the higher laws and higher authorities. Furthermore, intelligent human beings are free by definition, by status, and by rights.

You may claim any status that you desire including the intelligent human status, just by not claiming otherwise, in any form, verbal or written. You are considered in this manner to have an intelligent human status by all higher laws, and therefore implicitly by lower laws as it is the case with all laws here on Earth. And the higher laws are well respected today here on Earth in all jurisdictions, or at least they are respected everywhere within the West. If you wonder why you have to form separate identities in order to get all licenses and identities, to give your signature for everything involving business, money, property, banking, and employment, it is because you exit the jurisdiction of the higher laws only when you use these, only when you assume your consensual corporation written in uppercase letters. And once you exit the high jurisdiction of the higher laws, you lose all your human rights, because that consensual corporation is not a human nature but it is exactly the identity of a corporation. While corporations are dead bodies, as they have the status and rights of dead bodies, which is the first consensual level.

This explains a large amount of your consensual behavior

that you have to undergo throughout life, and this specific consensual behavior may be exploited legally by anyone who can and who knows exactly how to obey the higher laws. In fact, this entire enterprise of exploiting genuine living human beings as livestock and slaves in an enterprise spanning an entire world and an entire reality cannot take place without the higher laws, since through the entire bureaucracy, the higher laws back up this entire enterprise as being accurate, and it stands behind the Elite and behind all those who control the Elite, to defend them whenever they are challenged for infringing people's rights.

And this is how, these higher laws spanning the wider world and meant to protect all intelligences everywhere ever are turned around and are used against all intelligences everywhere. Yet this is not always the case, because all it takes is for you to assume your natural, living human nature that you have implicitly since birth, and the higher laws apply to you, as you are considered a genuine living human being. And once this is the case, any higher being up there is allowed to intervene in your behalf, take your side and defend you in full agreement with the higher laws.

And all that you have to do in order to identify yourself as a natural, genuine, living, intelligent human being is not to identify yourself otherwise, as a corporation, because you are already assumed to be a genuine living human being, since this is what you actually are, human, intelligent, alive, and existent. Therefore, do not claim in any form and manner that you are otherwise, as you do when you claim that you are another being, the specific consensual being or corporation written in uppercase letters.

There are many ways to trick you to wave your natural human nature besides this corporation written in uppercase letters, the Romans found a way to claim that you are a dead body or a corporation by default when you are born, if your soul is not there with you. And now, every time you do not state that your soul is there with you, you are considered by specific jurisdictions as a dead body. This is why there are many types of jurisdictions around this world. And even so, just because your country uses a specific type of jurisdiction, this does not mean that you are judged and considered by it, since many courts and other jurisdictions are phony, an enactment, or a stage where you are made to play a specific role and make you agree with incriminating claims. And once you give your agreement, you are ready to be punished.

If you ever wonder why those in power do not kill everybody and take the entire world for themselves, since they have the power and the technology to do so many times over, it is because the higher laws do not allow them.

How exactly can you get your human rights? Who can give them to you? Your nation, judicial authorities, along with your constitution? No, not at all. You have your human rights since birth, since they are implicitly yours by nature. Because there is no other way, you have to have your rights to fulfill your needs and meanings, or you die otherwise. Your human rights are your rights as a living, intelligent being to fulfill all your needs and meanings, and since you are human, you may refer to them as human rights.

Not only you, but all living beings and all intelligences have similar rights, they have the right to fulfill their needs and therefore they have the right to behave according to their normal natural desire. You have your rights to fulfill your needs in this world and therefore to undergo your normal human behavior. More precisely, you have the right to eat, sleep, procreate, learn, develop, defend yourself, be part of society, and ascend in society. And you have these rights just because you were born in this world as a living human being.

These rights are stated throughout constitutions and religious records, yet they are always yours, regardless if they are stated anywhere or not. And you do not even have to claim them, because they are always yours. Unless you wave them by stating otherwise, that you are anything else but a living human being, as a consensual corporation.

While corporations are consensual, of the first level, because they are instated and assumed to exist as a body or as a corpore, only by agreement that this is the case. Because by agreement, you may decide now that the sky is yellow or that words mean anything else, and this is how all statutes of all jurisdictions are made, only for words to mean something else. Since when the judge asks you in court if you understand, or if you respect the court, it means that you under-stand, or that you stand under, and that you agree that that specific room is a consensual court, isolated from the rest of the real world, because it is a specific jurisdiction where all words have different meanings and where you must behave by different laws, beliefs, and ideologies. And now, when you respect the court, you respect all these agreements, at the first consensual level, and in the Consensual Matrix.

Since as you notice, the entire consensual is not actually made to create human harmony in life and in this world at the third intelligent human level, but to instate consensually or by agreement everything that is not the case in life and in the real world. With the sky being yellow included, and with the normal word 'understand' meaning to subdue to, or to belong to, even as a slave. Since this is why the consensual is not the accurate, making your entre first level consensual behavior improper for genuinely intelligent human beings. With all these courts, jurisdictions, districts, states, and corporations composing the current consensual society interfering directly with Life and with the real world.

This helps us with our model of the human behavior, since it helps us distinguish the real from the consensual, the accurate from the invalid and the consensual, the good from the bad, the meaningful behavior from the consensual behavior, and the allowed from the forbidden.

You notice your natural, higher right to feed yourself in any manner, including by farming, fishing, and hunting. You do not need licenses and permits for all these. However, if you claim not to be a living human being but a dead corporation, then you have to obtain the proper licenses to get your food, since dead and consensual bodies do not have the need for food in this world, and therefore dead bodies do not have the permission to get food in any manner. Besides, all food belongs to the living, through their animal and human rights. And this is why you need all these documents as a corporation in the current consensual society, because you are not to do anything without them, since you are not a living human being, while this world belongs to living human beings, and to free animals.

Because as a living human being, you have the right to eat, recover, make shelters, travel, learn, and develop, and you may do all these without the use of laws, documents, and authorities. Therefore, you have the right to undergo your normal behavior, and I refer to it as your human behavior, or third level intelligent human behavior. Which is different from your first level consensual behavior.

While now, you are capable to distinguish between your consensual behavior and your human behavior. Take your time now to identify where and when you use the two types of behavior, and in what amount.

Since as you notice, in this human world, made by our Creator, for us the living human beings, in his correspondence, and given the right by our Creator to roam this world in any manner we please, we are allowed to undergo our actual human behavior only at home in private, but not exactly in the rest of this world. While officially, by law, all these restrictions address only the consensual corporations, which are not living human beings, and only within consensual jurisdictions, but not in the real world. Because officially, the current consensual society never interferes with Life, the real world, and our Creator and his intentions. Yet nobody cares about all these, behaving as slaves the entire time, Masses and Brotherhood alike. And in this manner, through this specific first level consensual behavior, they hand in the entire world to those of the social class above, the Elite. And they do so by creating specific social niches allowing the tyrants and dictators of this world to exploit this world through this entire first level servitude consensual behavior coming from everybody in this world.

We may identify now the consensual human behavior that creates the consensual social niche allowing those above to control society even implicitly, consensual niche that gives away everything to those above that control society. Just take away all natural human needs, meaning, and behavior, and you are left with the consensual behavior, consensual needs and meaning, consensual niche, and with the consensual environment. And this is what they never teach in school and state on TV or over the Internet, with the Brotherhood knowing some of it.

As a living human being, you are allowed to roam freely in order to fulfill your needs. And since everything that you do in life is fulfilling needs, you are allowed to travel anywhere at any time, even on public roads, since all public roads belong to the public, or to the people. You do not even need IDs and passports, since as a genuine living human being, you are the primary reference or primary witness, and you may state your identity as a genuine living intelligent human being at any time. You may claim so with everything that you ever claim as a primary reference, overruling everything else.

There are still some details. If you travel with the intention to do business or to buy anything, even food, then your living nature could be challenged, since money is consensual and it already belongs directly to the Family owning your specific nation. These also own you, your corporation. Once you use their money, then everything that you do, you do on their behalf, through your corporation. And therefore, they may forbid you to fulfill your natural needs through their money.

As religious records state, money is the mark of the devil, from the word 'mark,' which means stamp, and you cannot buy anything without it, obviously. And since you carry the money, you are owned by it, you are owned by the devil, and therefore you belong to the devil. These are not simple beliefs, but they are accurate.

And this is how they may trick you to wave your human rights while you are using their money, just because money is an agreement, between you and them, agreement done through your corporation, while agreement means consensus. Yet in any circumstance, as long as you remain within your natural niche, as long as you remain within your natural environment, and as long as you maintain your intelligent human nature, then you as a primary witness may overrule any claim anyone can make, just because they maintain their consensual existence throughout their entire interaction with you, while you are a living human being. And they may overrule you only as long as you are a consensual corporation yourself. But once you maintain your living human nature, you are incompatible, they cannot interact with you, and must close all statements, acts, and processes with you.

Furthermore, since all jurisdictions and corporations are instated in this world consensually, for the only meaning to serve the living human beings, you may require all corporations interacting with you in all jurisdictions to help you fulfill your needs, since you are a living human being. You may ask for food, shelter, transportation, water, comfort, and safety. Yet you cannot ask for money, since money is consensual.

The problem is that you cannot remain within your own natural niche, since you do not have one anymore. The current consensual society expanded globally, and took over your niche. You cannot eat anything within big cities and anywhere else, since you have to buy your food there. Therefore, you are never considered an intelligent human being within cities, but a corporation. The cities themselves are corporations and they are owned similarly by families, nations, religious entities, and banking entities. And this is the problem, because all these entities, all these consensual dead bodies have expanded to own and control everything in this world, the entire ecosystem, taking over the entire human niche.

As stated, your own natural niche is not available anymore, and you have to live in society, obey, play your role of a dead corporation, get your licenses, get your job, get your money, fulfill your needs, undergo your consensual behavior, keep all these consensual laws and schemes instated in society, and through them, keep this entire consensual niche instated throughout this world, probably indefinitely. While making possible all these tyrants and dictators throughout the upper social layers of this world, in the West and in the East. And with them fighting now for world supremacy in yet another world war, good luck to you.

What can you do? Everything depends on your developmental level. At your zero developmental level, you care less of any of these, as long as you have your drinks, smokes, dust, and pills. At the first consensual developmental level, you are already part of this entire Consensual Matrix spanning society, this world, and most of the wider world, enslaving everybody directly, including you and your family. Yet as cattle or slave, you still have your privileges and your minimum income guaranteed, and therefore you may still fulfill your needs and subsist. What happens is that as cattle and mostly as a slave, you are better off than the rest of the people, since you are part of this consensual scheme and you draw a profit alongside the rest of the social hierarchy, as small as it may be. Or this is the stereotype while underdeveloped.

At your second developmental level, you still care less about all these, as long as you are able to fulfill your basic needs, and therefore as long as you are able to subsist. In fact, it does not really matter what kind of society you are part of, since at your second animal intuitive developmental level, you will always behave in any manner allowing you to fulfill your animal needs, aggressively or not.

Only from the third intelligent developmental level up, people stop using their dead, consensual corporation in order to maintain their human status and human rights while exiting the Consensual Matrix, just because the intelligent human needs stop you from harming others directly and indirectly.

And it may seem unbelievable, but through your consensual behavior and particularly through your use of money, you are eating the food of all starving children from the poor nations, and they die because of you, because you afford to eat their food and they do not. Because food, money, and all basic resources are limited in this world, and when some people get more, others are left with less.

And this is the case because food is kept on lower levels on purpose, by discarding large quantities of it in every manner, in order for people to lack food and consequently to engage competitively one against another. You should see how milk is dumped in the sewer in very large quantities only to keep people underdeveloped and the current consensual society instated.

And if it is still unbelievable, search pictures and videos from the great recession over one century ago, to see not only people drastically malnourished, dying in large numbers of starvation and sickness, but also food being discarded and destroyed in very large quantities, to make the entire great recession possible. Back then, they called it stabilization of the market price of food, and so they destroyed all food, killing people by the millions, and ruining everybody. With the invisible kingdom profiting the entire time, as it took over the West. Over one century ago.

The invisible kingdom is an actual nation, originating in Georgia from the Caucasian region in Asia. The invisible kingdom migrated in mass to Europe and then to America, gradually taking over the West. While currently, the dictators of the East expand faster in this world, compared to the invisible kingdom, being more capable, and ready to defeat the invisible kingdom in yet another world war. Yet the invisible kingdom is worthless, hiding behind the native European genetic lines the entire time, losing the entire world to the East. And when this happens, you have dictatorships spanning this world in a global dynasty, and you go back to the Dark Ages.

Yet food is also part of your natural human niche and environment, and therefore the wide availability of food in this world may allow you to discard your consensual corporate identity, and assume your intelligent human nature, allowing you in this manner to escape society and live an intelligent human life. Yet even if you do so, you cannot eat the current food produced by society, because it is contaminated with additives that kill your cognitive system, and you cannot reason at the intelligent human level accurately enough to be able to generate, identify, and fulfill intelligent human needs. And then you have to watch TV, go to work, drink coffee and take the rest of the drugs, because this is what is left for you to do.

If all or a majority of people discard their consensual corporation, reclaiming their natural, intelligent human living nature along with their human status and human rights, to live within an intelligent human society, then they have a chance to make a change in this world for the better. Or they have a chance until they are compromised in any manner, by anyone living life on lower levels, anyone found either within or outside this new, developed society.

Because you have to be already developed at the third level in order for the new, developed society to be sustainable. In the overall human family, all goods, values, and resources should be shared in common and not in private by the entire society.

Yet do not rush up to open your front door to everyone in this world, since you harm yourself and your family if you do so. Because currently, the people of this world are underdeveloped, and cannot form the intelligent human family spanning this world. From lack of development. While you cannot constrain anyone to develop either.

Because as long as you take drugs at the zero developmental level, and as long as you serve continuously at your first consensual level, you cannot form the intelligent human society at the third intelligent level.

You may always develop yourself to the third intelligent human level as you do now while reading this book, but you cannot constrain anyone to develop, since they have to do so on their own, by fulfilling their own natural higher human developmental needs, exactly as you do now by reading this book. Since as always stated, you may always develop on your own, while hoping that the rest of this world does the same. And if it does not, then too bad for this world. But with the entire world constrained now with wars and dictatorships, which are possible only at an underdeveloped level, then too bad for this world.

Since only as long as everybody is developed at the intelligent human level, behaving at the intelligent human level, through the fulfillment of their intelligent human needs and meanings, they are capable to develop their environment and maintain it at the intelligent human level, with the intelligent human society included, or the overall human family. Until then, enjoy the wars, dictatorships, and pandemics.

And if you actually went through dictatorships yourself, you find these significant, since they are common behavior under dictatorships. If not, imagine conducting your entire private behavior at home in your family by laws strictly imposed. You are not a free living being anymore, but you are under oath, while you end up refraining yourself from tending to everybody else through your own needs and feelings, but by law. You lose your love for those who mean the most in your life, since now you fulfill consensual laws and duties. Even more, since you have to share equally everything in the family because this is what the law states, when you come home from shopping, you simply divide all groceries among yourselves, and you take them to your rooms. Similarly, you have precise schedules to share the TV and the bathroom, you split all expenses equally, and you watch everything that you say, because you are always judged accordingly, and punished by law.

How exactly are the normal human families that people have at home if they are not even equal, if you do not even share everything equally, since as you already know, you always take all the groceries to the refrigerator and to the cabinets and everybody eats normally? The difference is that at home, in your family, you do not actually share everything equally as everyone actually deserves, but you actually tend to everybody's needs directly, through your own needs and feelings, since your own intelligences send you the needs to tend to your loved ones just as you tend to yourself, through similar needs.

This is not exactly equality, but living harmony. And every

time you do so, your own intelligences reward you with love and happiness, which is your family fulfillment. Even more, this is why you call them your loved ones, since you feel love for them, since your own intelligences send you your love and happiness, for them.

And it is meaningful to keep them instated, through your intelligent human development. Since you do so for all the human needs, higher and lower, and not only for the need to eat. And this is why, once you introduce the beliefs and laws of any ideology and jurisdiction at home in the family, you lose your love and happiness, while you might even argue and ruin relationships, just because all beliefs and laws are consensual. While your family love and fulfillment is natural, it is alive. In other words, you cannot have natural behavior and consensual behavior simultaneously, at home, in society, in the Brotherhood, and in your community. While you cannot have even these small, isolated human families as they are today, since these demand a continuous human discrimination, but must have only the overall human family spanning this world, where everybody tends to the needs of everybody.

While all living beings behave in this manner, except for the human beings. While even humans lived in larger families, except for these centuries, and except for the times when the Consensual Matrix remains instated on Earth. And as you notice, the consensual human behavior ruins this world, taking humanity to its common grave.

Communism, capitalism, nationalism, socialism, and all the 'ism' in this world are social and political ideologies of the first consensual level, instated by agreement, while always twisted accordingly to allow all tyrants and dictators in this world, covertly or in the open, as you see these in the West and East. I cannot state which one is better, since at their first consensual level, they trash this world.

They took over society by expanding to cover the entire social niche of this world, while there is nothing left for you to do, and you have to limit yourself to what it is given to you by default. Yet be thankful for that little minimum income guaranteed if you happen to have one, because it can still feed you and your children. Because there are countries where people do not have it, they get sick, and many times, they die.

They forced you out of their way, and now they force you to work hard throughout life in order to create for them not only this consensual, abundant niche at their disposal, but to create an entire abundant, comprehensive consensual environment, which you create yourself alongside the rest of the Masses, through your work and through your social behavior in general. And they force you to behave in this manner mostly by keeping you busy, poor, ignorant, sick, weak, misfortunate, disconnected, incapable, guilty, and underdeveloped, regardless if you are from the Masses or the Brotherhood.

You might argue that if you are from the Brotherhood, you are never busy, sick, poor, and ignorant, since you have your prestige in the Brotherhood, yet all these are relative, while you could have significantly more in a comprehensive human family, where you maintained the harmony with everybody else, and did not even divide the people into social classes.

Society is controlled, and everybody knows it. Everybody knows that there are highly powerful and very wealthy people in this world, working together, consensually. There are also societies and organizations comprising an entire social class, the middle social class, the current consensual Brotherhood, which is serving in every manner these highly powerful individuals, the Elite, controlling today everything on their behalf: industry, business, science, medicine, commerce, and education. And as an individual, you stand no chance while competing socially or financially with the current Brotherhood itself, unless you are part of it. Because they work together, they profit together, and they share the profit. All being done at the expense of those competing individually, the Masses.

Social classes and social layers might seem normal to you, since this is what you learn in school, but when you study them closely, you notice how any divided hierarchical society is made in this manner to enhance social exploitation and social eradication, form the bottom social layers up.

Since it is only a social scheme, meant to assure continuous profit to those above, at the expense of those below. And this matches all social hierarchies spanning society from its bottom to the top.

Because this social division always happens in consensual environments, leading to wars of supremacy, genocide, and extinction. Because you cannot have Life and consensual behavior simultaneously, since the two remain incompatible, because consensual behaviors never fulfill Life, but they go against Life. And once you stop fulfilling Life, she discards you, and you clear the niche to allow anything or anyone else to take your place, regardless of species, nation, ideology, or social status.

Sociology divides society in three social classes: the poor, the middle class, and the rich. Different nations use different names for these classes, as the intellectuals, the aristocracy, the peasants, the commons, or the working class, but the idea is the same everywhere, since you always have these three social classes: the bottom social class, the middle social class, and the top social class.

There are specific income levels stating precisely where you are positioned in society. If you are making over one hundred thousand dollars a year, you may find yourself in the top social class, among the very rich. Yet you hear rumors about the one percent of this world holding ninety-nine percent of the wealth in this world. Therefore, when you do the math, it does not match what sociology states. Even more, of you are from the bottom social class and become rich suddenly ascending to the top social class officially, you do not control this world at all along with the rest of the rich. Which means that the model for the human society that sociology teaches is inaccurate, hiding something.

There are hidden social classes in society, comprising people that you will never see, meet, or hear about, people that live entirely above money, people that are served and venerated as deities, people so powerful, that their slaves and servants are the richest and the most powerful people that society allows you to know. I refer to this specific hidden, top social class as the Elite. Right below them is the current consensual Brotherhood, which is the middle social class, comprising all powerful organizations as the masons, along with all business cartels, religious organizations, criminal organizations, political organizations, and royalties. These are the ones serving the Elite in every manner, while the Elite keep them in power above the Masses. And the Masses are the bottom social class.

More precisely, if you compete in the current society alone or within your small family and entourage of friends, you are in the Masses. But if you compete in the current society within an entire organization, as an entire criminal organization, religious ideology, political party, masons, business cartel, or knights, then you are in the middle social class, the Brotherhood. While the Brotherhood is legal and illegal, with the people from the current legal Middle Brotherhood owning the criminal brotherhood entirely.

The Brotherhood is not secret, but only its entire activity in the world is kept secret. Which is the case with both the legal and the illegal Brotherhood. This is why you never see the Brotherhood in all news and movies, since the entire activity of the Brotherhood in the world is secret. Or at least secret from the Masses. Which is tremendous endeavor of secrecy, considering that this entire world is in the Brotherhood, legal or illegal. While above the Brotherhood, the Elite is secret, along with its entire presence and activity in the world. While the Masses are the masses.

As a short reference, the Italian Mafia acted freely in Italy for a very long time, while only in the seventies, some journalist or police investigator 'discovered' the Mafia. While the Mafia engulfed and made use of the entire Italy, and everyone knew of it, tens of millions of people, as these lived their lives entirely in the Mafia. While there was nothing in the news, movies, books, newspapers, and magazines about Mafia. But that police investigator worked hard and fought hard to 'discover' the Mafia, which was the entire Italy, making its presence known to the world. And it is the same with the entire Brotherhood, and not only about Mafia, which is always in the Brotherhood.

Within the Brotherhood, you also have the invisible kingdom, which actually controls the entire Brotherhood tightly, or this is the case in the West. Because in the East, you have entire political parties, religious ideologies, alphabet agencies, and business cartels controlling tightly the Brotherhood of the East. With the Brotherhood of the West and the Brotherhood of the East in a continuous cooperation, forming one Brotherhood, and therefore one middle social class. With the Elite of this world intermarried in one large prosperous human family, while served diligently by the Higher Brotherhood.

Now, if you truly make over one hundred thousand a year, you must be in the Brotherhood yourself, within the Lower Brotherhood, not in the Masses, and certainly not in the Elite. Since the Brotherhood manages all well-paid jobs and all successful businesses as it pleases, your highly paid job is also managed by the Brotherhood. You serve them well, and in exchange, they allow you to keep your job. And so you get to make one hundred grant a year, while doing everything that they demand, everything they order. And with all organizations within the Brotherhood continuously cooperating with each other, the Brotherhood spans this world in all domains. The Brotherhood controls this world including all sides of all wars simultaneously, and nothing is natural within the social environment anymore, since they control everything, including space exploration and world starvation, the level of science and the type of motor that you have in your car.

As a reference, presidents and ex-presidents are somewhere in the Middle Brotherhood, while the Rockefellers are by the top of the Higher Brotherhood.

Who exactly are you and where exactly are you positioned within society? It is not as conspiracy theories state, that if you ever want to get rich you simply join the Brotherhood, you get rich fast, and then you see all your dreams come true, while you wreck this world together in the process. Yet you may always wreck this world together in the process, but if you are not born in the Brotherhood, it is more likely that you never get to join the Brotherhood. Or you may join the Lower Brotherhood, the very bottom of the Lower Brotherhood. Even so, you get to hold an employment guaranteed or a small business, you get to be friends with the bosses at work, while you do not get speeding tickets anymore, since you know all the signs. You will get to see and do a lot in the Lower Brotherhood, so you may have a large amount of stories to tell, if you were only allowed to talk.

But in general, you tend to live your life within the social class where you were born, unless this world order changes on you, which happens often. About duties, sometimes the orders that you receive are very favorable to you, privileging you beyond your expectations. Yet some other times, they may be unfavorable, and you have to sell shares suddenly, sell successful businesses to specific people, relocate, defeat and destroy others, destroy even good friends of yours in any manner, and much more, since you live your life under oath continuously.

Within the Brotherhood, you live your brotherhood life at the first level, in servitude. The bottom part of the Brotherhood serves the top, while the top part of the Brotherhood serves directly the Elite.

About the Elite, well, no one talks about the Elite. The Masses do not even know about the Elite, and this is exactly why, when the Masses take to the street to riot and protest against anything for any reason, they do not even know against whom to protest. Because the Masses have to use the knowledge about society that sociology feeds to them, so they revolt against the top social class depicted by the current sociology, which is the rich, the ones making over one hundred thousand a year, as the doctors, the lawyers, and the politicians, since these are the only rich people in this world that they know and are available. Because the extremely rich people that they see on TV, those must be in Monte Carlo or in Bahamas, and they cannot go to protest there, because they have to be at work in the morning. So people usually protest against dentists and stockbrokers, they turn their own cars upside down and they charge the police, and then they go home. The Lower Brotherhood may know what is going on in this world, yet the Lower Brotherhood must show reliability to those above, so they never talk about anything hidden or forbidden.

What is trivial to see is that the current hierarchic Brotherhood seems to be more capable and more powerful than the Elite. How can the Elite remain in power? The Elite was eliminated many times by the Brotherhood and by the Masses, yet when we consider power and influence in this model, we should consider everything, including higher behavior and higher abilities. Because while the Masses and the Brotherhood are expected to ridicule and avoid everything related to higher abilities, higher influence, and higher knowledge, the Elite accumulates these in every manner, because higher powers of any kind makes the difference between being followed as an ordinary president by those immediately below you, or being venerated as a genuine deity by the entire world, dynasty after dynasty, hidden or in the open. And it is through this type of higher powers that the Elite manages to keep the Brotherhood instated in society over the Masses, and it is through this same higher powers that the Elite subdues the Brotherhood and keeps it under control, many times drastically.

Yet the Brotherhood and the Masses enter in possession of higher powers from time to time, higher artifacts and higher abilities, and so the wheel of history turns and turns, revolution after revolution. Until now, because now the Elite has the necessary knowledge and technology to make the Masses and Brotherhood destroy themselves and leave this world altogether. And it happens, slowly but steadily.

Today, the Elite are a genuine large human family, with their few genetic lines already intermarried in a single one. It is rumored that the Elite have already divorced society, and now they live as an independent, runaway society, or even as an independent civilization. Whatever the case is, the Elite must still be served and supplied with work and resources of every kind by the other social classes, the Brotherhood and the Masses. If not, they have to work on every domain of their new civilization: agriculture, industry, construction, or mining.

This entire consensual social niche matrix that the Masses and the Brotherhood create throughout life and society is meant to sustain this entire separate civilization made by the Elite. And it will continue to sustain them while they commit genocide in every manner by killing entire genetic lines one after another from the bottom layer of society up, all the way to the Higher Brotherhood. And if it takes them years to kill society in this manner, they certainly have the time to wait, because it is rumored that they live very long lives.

Who serves whom and who works for whom in society? Society has a well-defined hierarchy of power, wealth, and influence, called this world order. Society is formed by smaller social layers, covering all its classes. Through hierarchy and agreement, each social layer serves the immediate top layer, which serves its top layer, up to the Elite. What we notice today, and what we always encounter is a continuous clash between two factions, as these compete for supremacy. The West and the East. These clashes may involve the entire society in their fight, since everyone wants to take sides and to share the victory if they win, and advance socially. Yet most of the time, you are ordered to participate in the fight, along with all the wealth and influence that you have.

Why having clashes? While living life underdeveloped, the entire world is involved in social competition at all levels and in all domains, from large corporations to little kindergartens, everybody competes and fights. Yet sometimes, within the Upper Brotherhood, entire lower social layers become more capable than top social layers. They challenge and overtake each other throughout the fight, overruling upper layers and therefore advancing socially by force, while changing the entire world order into the new world order.

And this goes on in this world right now, and you hear

important people everywhere threatening each other with words as 'the new world order,' and with 'and we will have it,' but the other side says 'no, you will never have it.' The West against the East. While the outcomes are already agreed within the Elite of the West and the East, to have an overall dynasty in this world, with them in control, when they can rule in the open, as true dictators. Or deities, as they call themselves.

Since this is what you serve throughout your entire consensual behavior, and this takes most of your life. Therefore, you are more a consensual corporation throughout your existence than a living human being, for these people to trash this world, with you doing the trashing for them. And them keeping this world, since they blame you for trashing it and they take it from you, and this is the current hierarchic consensual human society. For as long as it lasts.

You may find these highly significant social movements to be random or inevitable, as a built-up of social steam, yet these may become predictable, once you understand them. Because it is always the new money challenging the old money. Today, the new money is the Internet, while only last century or so, the new money used to be oil. The Rockefellers won the fight then, along with everyone still in power today around this world. Google, Amazon and the rest are the new money today. And therefore, the Families owning these have to advance today within the Middle Brotherhood, as they accumulate wealth and influence.

What is to notice here is that both the old money and the new money are within the invisible kingdom, or this is the case at least in the West. Whatever the case is, it is always technology offering a new method of gathering wealth form the lower society, as rubber and oil did in the past, and as computers, Internet, and online activity do more recently. New methods of accumulation of wealth are what always change the balance of power, capabilities, wealth, influence, and aspirations within distinct factions of the upper part of society, and this is how they compete.

And now, how exactly do you want the Internet to change

its policies and link computers not to central servers, but one to another, bypassing Google, Facebook, and Amazon, while this is how these giants make their wealth, through centralized online activity, and not through independent, individual, free online activity?

As you notice, life is not as plentiful and as secure within the upper social classes as they advertise in conspiracy theories. The Elite is highly vulnerable through its supreme position in society. The Brotherhood has overruled and replaced the Elite repeatedly throughout history, and this may happen again in your lifetime, with you never noticing, it if you are not there. There are currently even members of the Masses within the Elite, the Rothschilds, and they entered it only this century. Entire families of the Brotherhood are vulnerable, since the Lower Brotherhood is highly capable and highly anxious for fight and victory, siding with anyone who makes promises, and playing it rough. While with each larger revolution, the Masses overturned both the Brotherhood and the Elite at once, whenever these remained in the open, not hidden.

Yet no matter who overturns whom, who wins entire wars and revolutions and who loses them, these three social classes will always exist in a hierarchic, consensual world, only with different social actors animating them. Because nothing changes in a consensual world regardless of how many revolutions are fought, and this is the case because societies of the first consensual level as the current human society are highly stable and highly rewarding, for those in control and for their long hierarchy of servants and slaves underneath.

Why having this strong social stability at the first developmental level, mostly when entire wars and revolutions are fought mainly to free the people from merciless tyrants, political thefts, and opportunistic profiteers? Why does this world fall back into tyranny and oppression after every revolution, with all tyrants freshly removed every time? Because this world is never divided into good people and bad people as you see in the news, as you learn in school, and as you see in the movies, with the bad always engaging the good, they fight for some time and then the good ones win. Because everybody is the same in this world, and more importantly, everybody is good. People of this world were supposed to live life as genuinely developed humans within an intelligent human society forming an intelligent human civilization, but they got what we have today.

Because otherwise, the tyrants throughout the upper social layers are not possible. Revolutions will always follow revolutions because society will always be divided into the steady Masses, the serving Brotherhood, and the supreme Elite, regardless of their members. And this is the case just because the entire world will always assure this specific consensual niche to remain open in this world endlessly, and to allow this extraordinary social hierarchy to form, with lower social layers serving higher social layers, endlessly.

And it is the entire world forming and maintaining this specific consensual social niche that keeps society at the first consensual level because this is a first level consensual niche in itself, having all the necessary first level niche elements: sentientism, egoism, nationalism, communism, socialism, and capitalism, fueled by direct, strong needs for money, hierarchic domination, and pleasure at all costs.

You notice how the need for money, the need for domination, and the need for pleasure are only consensual needs, yet they feed directly on your natural needs, since the fulfillment of these three needs assure you the fulfillment of all natural needs that you will ever have, endlessly. Money buys resources for your lower needs, while pleasure from drugs and entertainment can hack directly into your punishment-reward mechanism to keep you happy endlessly, regardless if you fulfill your needs or not, since you are never punished with pain, boredom and depression. Similarly, hierarchic domination ensures the successful fulfillment of all your social and reproductive needs. Your subconscious is happy with these three consensual needs throughout life, you are happy when your subconscious rewards you continuously, you strive to keep society at its first consensual level, and this is how you keep this specific social niche open. With the rest of society doing the same.

In other words, it does not matter who you are, because once you decay to your zero and first developmental levels, if the need that you receive is to remain a dictator endlessly, regardless of how many people you harm in the process, this is exactly what you do, and you remain a dictator for life.

Because this world is never divided into the good and the bad, since everybody is just the same. Do you want to be and remain good throughout life, guaranteed? Then make sure that you remain developed, educated, and free of drugs continuously, because it is enough for you to lose any one of your human niche elements, and you lose control, you decay, you lose your intelligent human behavior, you cannot get back to the third level because your human environment is already compromised, your cognitive system is also compromised many times irremediably, and you certainly become bad. Or you become what society currently calls 'bad,' because as you see, from the higher perspective of Life herself, there is nothing bad in this world, but everything ends up in her favor. And there is nothing bad with you either, because everything that you ever do ends up good and favorable for her.

Can first level consensual societies be better, more stable, and more efficient than higher level ones? First level consensual societies are more stable than animal societies, which tend to be more chaotic and more unpredictable. Yet third level intelligent human societies are more efficient, more prosperous, and longer lasting. Because first level consensual societies last only until the next cataclysm.

Cataclysms come in levels, from one to ten. First level consensual civilizations may survive cataclysms of the first level and lower, while third level intelligent human civilizations survive third level cataclysms, as larger asteroids impacting Earth, super volcanoes, pole shifts, and very large solar flares. The larger the cataclysm, the more developed a civilization must be in order to be able to cope with it. As a civilization, you need highly advanced knowledge in order to avoid cataclysms, or you need highly advanced social orders to survive in mass once you cannot avoid them. And with people undergoing first level behaviors for life within first level societies, being drugged and entertained continuously while learning and achieving nothing, you have no chance for success. And then, after major cataclysms, even developed societies may fall back to their first or second developmental levels, and so you end up where you started, at the first consensual servitude level. It is always the first level, because the first level niche is always open, since people just keep it open, as it is the case in most of the wider world, since this is the Consensual Matrix.

But why exactly underdeveloped people form and keep this consensual niche open, allowing all tyrants and dictators to use it, while keeping this world controlled and exploited? Everybody keeps the consensual niche open in this world through their needs of the first level, since it is easier to fulfill all basic needs through first level needs. Because the entire first level society provides for you, with you having only to obey orders or to make money. And if you ever have problems, authorities help you, and they show you what to do. So your successful fulfillment of all your needs is almost guaranteed.

How exactly does your subconscious know what needs to send to you and when? And then, at a closer study, is it not your subconscious keeping society stuck at the first consensual level? Are intelligences actually able to affect society directly, right from within your cognitive system? And about your intelligences, how exactly can they send you your needs, in such a precise manner? And how exactly do you develop and decay? What exactly happens? Yet questions are many to ask here, and they seem to be of a cognitive nature now. I have kept these first chapters on objective, social, consensual, and empirical levels, for you to be able to understand the setting, the objective structure of our model of the human behavior. We are switching now perspectives to model needs, reasoning, and intelligences as they determine directly your behavior.

5 YOUR COMPLEX INTELLIGENT BEHAVIOR

As seen, your lifeline of causality is crowded with activity and events, determining and controlling your physical behavior, while comprising your cognitive or subjective behavior. Your needs and thinking determine and control your physical behavior, while your needs and thinking are in themselves your cognitive, subjective behavior. In order to understand and be able to control your cognitive behavior, which is the behavior of all your intelligences including you the conscious intelligence, you must be able to model and therefore understand the human reasoning, the human cognition, and the human intelligences. One problem with understanding reasoning is that you have to employ reasoning in order to understand reasoning. This is how you cannot understand reasoning in an empirical manner, through observation, because you enter a loop of reasoning that can mislead you. You cannot do so mathematically either, nor technologically. This is why science remains incapable to understand and explain reasoning, because science is empirical entirely, and rather primitive and backwards in research methods, concepts, and ideas.

Psychology studies behavior in order to model reasoning. This is a backwards type of empirical study, and logically erroneous. We cannot use this method either, because we model behavior itself and therefore we enter another loop of reasoning. We are going to make our model for the human cognitive behavior from scratch, starting with the most basic structures determining and forming reasoning in all intelligences. Everything is related, interconnected, and is one. Therefore, if you want to understand the human reasoning, you have to understand everything related to thoughts, intelligences, and reasoning taking place everywhere and at all time. You have to understand entire lines of causality, you have to study and understand what describes them and how they manifest, and you have to do so within entire pertinent models of study. Otherwise, you end up inventing and assuming irrelevant causes for your observed events as psychology does, and this is invalid research. And then when you force an entire army of scientists and an entire society to accept your assumptions as accurate facts, then it is called dogma.

I refer to the human thinking as reasoning, since it is more complex, it is a third level intelligent thinking. As a reference, zero level thinking is random, monotone, invalid, addicted, vicious, or disabled. First level thinking is based entirely on basic algorithms, as if-then and repeat-until basic logical algorithms. We find this first level thinking in computers, mechanisms, machines, and in basic servitude thinking, when you follow orders exactly as they come and exactly as you must. Thinking through beliefs is also a first level cognitive behavior. Following procedures accurately is a first level thinking, along with following ideologies of any nature. This is why first level people and first lever societies are of the first consensual level, because they follow a first level consensual, procedural thinking. Technicians are of the first level in their domain, along with servants, slaves, cattle, and members of hierarchies. Or they are of the first level as long as they are found in first level circumstances. Current social behavior demands a first level thinking since it is based mostly on following laws and orders and on doing what others do and think. You must obey these, or you are caught, judged, and punished if you do not, since the laws themselves constraining you are consensual.

Throughout life, you go to work, you make money, and you use it to fulfill needs, and nothing else. If you are ever stuck and do not know what to do, you do not have to employ higher level reasoning, because you are helped in every manner by your authorities. Yet this is the case in principle, because in practice, everything is done against you in society. It takes you an intense human reasoning only to be able to dodge the menaces of society, if you happen to live an independent life and you are not in the system yourself, within social hierarchies.

Second level thinking is the animal thinking, and it involves the basic logical procedures if-then and repeat-until of the first level algorithmic consensual thinking, along with the intuitive cognitive procedures of the second level thinking, called intuitive thinking.

Intuition is second level thinking, it is not consensual, and it is based on continuously improved cognitive repetition, intuitive cognitive behavior that we have already seen in the past chapter. This repetitive, persistent intuitive cognitive development is called instinctual learning, yet there is more to learning to consider. It is relevant to state that it takes a complex nervous system as a brain, to be capable enough to offer the cognitive procedures necessary at least for intuitive thinking.

Third level thinking or human reasoning is based on complex, abstract conceptual learning and on complex mental modeling. Humans also use the first level algorithmic thinking along with the animal intuition of the second level throughout their reasoning. What adds to the human cognition is an abstract conceptual language that is capable to understand and define abstract conceptual terms defining all environmental elements and details, to use them in learning and throughout reasoning. Abstract conceptual terms used in abstract conceptual mental models may generate abstract ideas, while abstract ideas make the difference between the human behavior and animal behavior. And this is the case because these abstract ideas enable humans to do everything of an objective nature, including changing their objective, material environment as they please. How does everything take place from a cognitive perspective? Why do humans have to reason throughout life? Why do they have to learn? Let us see.

Humans have to fulfill needs. This fulfilling behavior remains of the first level as long as the environment does not change, since all human intelligences know exactly where all resources are, and they know exactly how to determine you to behave in order to go get them. Problems arise when the environment changes and you have to find other ways to fulfill your needs. Your behavior may shift to the second level if the problem is not too bad. At the second level, you use your intuitive thinking, you find the box of cereal because it was in the other bedroom after all, you had looked for it around the house twice and you finally found it, now everything is fine, and you may have your breakfast because you are not that late. It could have been worse.

For example, you were back from work and you had no food in the house, and no money, and now you had to find a way to get food fast before you left for your second job, because you are already late. You have to model your entire feeding procedure in your mind, how you have to pass by the bank first, get cash, stop by a restaurant, and eat there fast. But you are late for work, and everything takes too much time in your model, so your mental model fails. You start another mental model, you drive directly to a restaurant, pay with the credit card, you imagine not being able to find a parking spot because it is rush hour, you try to find another restaurant in your mind, and you keep reasoning at the third intelligent level. The first part of your mental model is finished, so you are ready to leave, hoping to finish your model on your way to work in order to get something to eat. You start behaving for real now, you leave the house, you get in the car, and drive.

Then you stop to pick up your food because you had managed to find the fastest way, you eat it while you drive, and you get to work just in time, everything according to your intense modeling.

And this is intelligent human reasoning of the third level, in a consensual world, and as you notice, it involves a multitude of abstract elements if you are from the Masses. Because if you were from higher social classes, your servants, which are also the Masses, did everything for you. And more importantly, did everything for you through similar complex mental models.

Why having advanced, higher level cognitive behavior present within lover level social layers? This is how they are milked, not exactly of workforce as they are made to believe, but of highly intelligent cognitive force. And it has to be in this manner, because the higher social levels cannot manage the unfavorable third level environment on their own. Otherwise, they simply used domestic animals, robots, machines, and computers, not living human beings. While the souls of the Masses have to become involved throughout this entire process. While this is higher level slavery, in a lower level consensual world. And it is very common in the Consensual Matrix.

Note how you would have never been able to get your food if not for your advanced mental model, which is third level intelligent reasoning. Because at the zero level thinking, you would have gotten a case of beer instead, called in sick, took the alcohol home and watched cable for the rest of the day to get you started for the party, since you had more drugs lined up, with very good friends to come and bring even more.

At the first level thinking, you would have left the house in a hurry, hoping to find something on your way to work to eat, but you found everything too crowded and you had no time to stop to eat. How misfortunate, you think, but with your first level thinking, you assume that it is not your fault that you remain hungry for the rest of the day. Therefore, now you have no reason to improve your thinking in any manner. And this is why first level thinking is so stable, mostly when society allows you to live life at the first level. Because there are always food machines with chips, chocolate, and cookies everywhere at work, and you may always eat that. While you are never capable to realize how harmful that food is, it keeps your thinking with a lower performance, and this is why first level thinking is so stable and so common in society.

There are many factors involved in keeping the extraordinary human brain performing at the first level of thinking, as powerful chemical substances found in food, drugs, drinks, and medicine, all harming you irreparably. There are powerful stereotypes invading your reasoning from everywhere, teaching you exactly how to think and behave at the first level and how to reject your human reasoning and behavior. And this is exactly what you do, since everybody does just the same. There are also the powerful social hierarchies engaging you, engulfing you, and forcing you to think and display the exact behavior that they seek, which is complete servitude, and these are of the first level. And your entire lifestyle is of the first level, and it is the only one, since this is what society offers to your social class.

Yet you can never tell these to anyone, because their lifestyle is their life and it is sacred to them. They get upset and they get mad on you when you challenge their dogma, beliefs, and thinking level. Or this is the case at a lower developmental level. Because genuinely developed humans are always eager to learn everything about themselves from other perspectives, just because they know that when they assess their reasoning through their own reasoning they enter loops of reasoning.

What loops of reasoning? People in a coma will remain in a coma because they assume everything to be real there, just because when they check reality, they check that specific reality of the coma but not the outer reality, and the coma reality seems to be real and reassuring every time they check. It is the same with addicted people or people of lower developmental level, because as long as their thinking remains impaired or at a very low level, they cannot realize the cognitive problem that they have, because thinking itself is compromised.

This is why it is always tedious to identify dogma and beliefs within your own reasoning and within your own memories, because you have to employ thinking based on these, and it may be accurate or not. Or you have to employ thinking based on common beliefs that are based on these, and you enter cognitive loops of reasoning in this manner, loops taking you nowhere while validating any assumption. And so you end up accepting invalid beliefs, compromising your entire cognitive system. And these are what I refer to as your consensual cognitive barbarian invaders, since they are capable to hijack your reasoning and you are down to lower levels of thinking, constrained by beliefs, stereotypes, strong personal convictions, ideologies, and jurisdictions.

Because you have to find separate ways to assess your own reasoning and memories, not through your own reasoning and memories as we have seen, because it may lead you nowhere. But through other people's perspectives, reasoning, and memories, which may also take you into loops of reasoning, into their loops of reasoning. Or you may compare your reasoning, knowledge, and your entire cognitive behavior with what specialized authorities claim to be accurate reasoning and beliefs in this world, yet these are of the first consensual level, rendering you consensual in a similar manner. You are altered on purpose, and meant to conduct your comprehensive behavior methodically and consensually on their behalf, serving them, since this is the name of the game.

What can you do? You have to seek pertinent, accurate knowledge to help you develop your reasoning and knowledge along with your entire cognitive behavior, but accurate knowledge is absent entirely, censored, denied, and destroyed, while the available knowledge is altered and consensual, serving directly corrupt authorities, since everything is interconnected in this world in a consensual manner, forming the Consensual Matrix, world after world.

And so there is no way for your to assess your own reasoning, to be able to distinguish the good from the bad yourself, yet you always have to find a way enabling you to distinguish between the good and the bad yourself, otherwise, you end up depending on harmful people, or depending on empty ideologies, or depending on mischievous, greedy authorities, while these are not at all favorable human conditions. And since unfavorable environmental conditions lead you away from your desired intelligent human behavior, then what do you do?

Nothing, since there is no way out, no solution, nothing at all. Unless you reconstruct the entre science yourself, through comprehensive mental models and entire research, as you find in this entire book series, which is extraordinarily tedious. Yet you still have to do so. And you have to do so only to understand your comprehensive environment in all its elements and details, including its favorable and unfavorable conditions. And since the environmental elements are formed through supreme natural laws, facts, and concepts, these lead you to the accurate truth, giving you the necessary accurate points of reference throughout a comprehensive reasoning at the intelligent human level and higher, to help you throughout your intelligent human behavior. Otherwise, you remain in the Consensual Matrix and you trash this world, world after world, as far and as long as the Consensual Matrix lasts.

Because this social system, this extraordinary profitable social enterprise is so mischievous, that most capable intelligences fall in it as flies, give in as kittens, and obey everything as slaves. And the more capable these higher beings are when they get here, the more they damage this world with everyone in it under the Consensual Matrix. And this is when the consensual enterprise becomes highly capable and highly profitable, while even more capable intelligences keep on falling in, as flies, age after age and world after world.

And everything happens because you cannot distinguish between the accurate and the consensual anymore once you get here as a higher being, as you cannot distinguish among all your realities when you are in a coma. Because if you are not capable to distinguish the good from the bad yourself, no one will do so for you, despite of what they may claim, since everything that they claim is meant for you to serve them.

This is always the case when it comes to beliefs, dogma, and ideologies. They corrupt your reasoning, and they subdue your natural intelligences. And this is how people of various cults, religions, and social or national ideologies end up engaging in horrific acts, which they consider to be entirely normal, entirely plausible, and entirely benefic. And this explains the wars and bad news that you see on TV while you take your food additives with your breakfast, never suspecting that there could be anything wrong with you and with this world in general. Probably because this world itself corrupts your reasoning and your entire cognitive behavior, while your food additives harm your brain to impair your mind to corrupt your reasoning and entire cognitive behavior.

The second level of thinking is the animal thinking and it includes intuition, along with the basic algorithms and stereotypes of the first level thinking. At the second level thinking, your second level behavior also kicks in, you drive fast and then you double-park in a hurry at the first restaurant, you go in front of the line and you demanded to be served for any invented reason, you lie, you beg, and you threaten, you do anything in order to get your food fast, and more importantly, you do everything that worked before, anything that you heard about from friends, anything that others did and it worked for them, anything that you found in movies and books. You try them until one solution works, and this is called intuitive thinking, because the next time, you will remember and you will try this specific successful method first.

Yet there is more to intuitive thinking, since intuitive thinking behavior is not so methodical, since this example is almost rational in nature, which is already third level intelligent thinking. The second level Intuitive thinking behavior is based many times on feelings, and this allows you to perform it with your subconscious intelligences directly. And this is the case because, at the second intuitive level, you store everything in your inner replica of this world through feelings, through specific feelings attached rigidly to everything that you know, understand, and remember. This is how you do not reason analytically or rationally at the second intuitive level, but you may only follow your feelings, and these take you there. And this is the case just because you have your feelings stored in your inner replica of this world, memorized there rigidly along with the actual memories. And now, when you have to decide at the intuitive level, you only follow your feelings, and you choose the best solutions according to your feelings.

And many times, this is your best choice, since it had brought the best success in the past along with the best feelings, and this is what you now choose. And as you notice, you perform this simple cognitive intuitive process or behavior through your conscious or subconscious intelligences, and this is your cognitive behavior of the second intuitive level.

Your cognitive second level intuitive behavior is different from your first level consensual cognitive behavior, since the first level cognitive behavior is consensual in nature and it follows laws, beliefs, strong personal convictions, stereotypes, ideologies, and entire jurisdictions, overruling your feelings and entire second level intuition, and many times, overruling even your third level rational cognitive intelligent human behavior, if you ever manage to conduct this.

Your subconscious intelligences also have their own thinking, cognitive behavior, and replicas of this world, as your subconscious intelligences reason there through similar mental models. Their inner replicas of this world are also of the second level, more direct and more efficient, being made of direct stimuli-response memory couples, cognitive mechanism that you interpret as reflexes. Yet your own feeling-memory couples is only one type of the general stimuli-response memory couples that you find throughout all second level cognitive realities or inner replicas of this world. This is how second level replicas of this world offer you solutions fast and directly, while all that you are left to do is simulate these fast, and so you choose the best.

In other words, while humans may have individual concepts, objects, and subjects in a third level inner replica of this world, subconscious intelligences may have logic cognitive couples, as spider - jump, and good food - eat. And they have a large amount of alternative plans, since this makes algorithmic thinking intuitive, as plan B, and plan C, always influencing their cognitive behavior.

Since as you already notice, while you perform your social behavior through your human organism, social self, and consensual corporation, you perform your cognitive behavior through your conscious intelligence, inner self, and the multitude of primal intelligences that use your own conscious inner replica of this world or they use their own subconscious inner replica of this world depending on their own specializations, and this is how all intelligences reason and behave cognitively in general. While you behave higher through your higher self and through its own higher cognitive behavior, now being your own higher cognitive behavior, if you can ever manifest this higher behavior in this world, and if you have a soul.

And as we always notice, you always have to behave through a different self of yours in each one of your separate realities, just because you cannot go there yourself as an organism, physical body, or living human being, you have to behave in this world through your physical body, organism, or living human being. Yet your life and existence do not stop in your natural environment, because you have to behave in the intelligent human society through your social self. Additionally, you have to behave in the Consensual Matrix through your consensual corporation, which is your brand or name written in uppercase letters, since this is now your consensual self. And many times, you are constrained to do so because your living human niche is not there anymore, and you cannot subsist as a physical self, the living human being.

And this is called living constraint or slavery, and this infringes the human rights, with no one even caring. Additionally, you have to behave in all your videogames and social media platforms through all your online videogame characters and social media avatars, just because as always seen, you cannot go into these computer worlds in living person, with your entire organism, but you have to have an avatar already existing there. Additionally, you have to behave cognitively within the multitude of mind worlds through your inner selves and intelligences as your conscious intelligence, inner self, and primal intelligences. And these count in zillions, each intelligence having its own inner replica of the outside world, with you as a conscious intelligence having your own inner replica of the real world, which is this conscious mind world where you now think, follow this book, imagine, decide, feel, believe, hope, analyze, and deduce. And who would have thought that the human behavior can be so complex?

As you notice, you have a multitude of realities where you undergo your multiple existence many times simultaneously, and you always do so through the multitude of your selves, one for each one of your realities. Because as always seen, you are not an individual living being, since Life, Intelligence, and existence can never manifest individually and distinctly for all details of an environment, but you are an entire lifeline of existence, containing all your selves on it, having them living one through another many times, with each one of your selves existing in their own separate reality. These are your selves and realities as a genuine living being, and as you notice, they think and behave independently, and many times, they do so one through another.

The second level intuitive cognitive behavior manifests when you have to choose fast among all these alternatives, since you have to choose the best, instantly. This act of choosing the best may seem deductive in nature yet it is not, since by having feelings embedded in your memories and in these stimuli-response memory couples in special, all that you have to do is consider the best feelings that you prefer to have as result, and that is what you choose, only to feel better.

And so you make your choice, you choose this new procedure of fulfilling your need from now on, and you are fine. If it happens to be wrong, then you miss your opportunity to feel good, and you regret it, while you go hungry, you fall sick, or you miss your partner. For all these you are punished, and you will certainly remember not to make the same decision the next time, since these bad feelings remain associated with this specific choice within your inner replica of this world. In other words, all these punishing feelings become associated with this specific stimuli-response memory couple, and you will not choose this specific response the next time, in order not to suffer, since all feelings are linked directly to your memories at the second, intuitive level. And this is called intuitive behavior, which is choosing your best way out through feelings.

Or you may behave in the outside world directly through entire associated similar subconscious reflexes, when you have no choice as a conscious intelligence, because now your primal subconscious intelligences consider it imminent enough to act in the outside world directly, overruling you the conscious intelligence. And this is how you scream, jump, run away, and vomit, subconsciously, by reflex. And it is still your behavior, your physical, objective behavior, but it is their cognitive intuitive behavior manifesting through the physical body, coming directly from your subconscious intelligence. And it happens through all your primal intelligences, as your reproductive, social, and security intelligences. And if these happen to live their lives at the second level, their behavior is animal or intuitive in nature, they manifest it directly in the real world through your physical self, and it becomes a real, objective behavior there.

And if your physical subconscious reflex behavior is harmful in any manner, by consensual standards, your consensual corporation may be blamed for it and could even have to go to jail and serve some time, while your physical body or the entire living human being has to go along with it to jail since this is the consensual agreement, to represent your consensual self in jail. And you have to bring along to jail your entire inner world filled with zillions of living intelligences including the conscious intelligence who do not want to be in jail since they cannot develop and reproduce in jail. Your higher self does not want it either, along with its own higher selves. And in this manner, everybody is thrown out of the way and cannot even reproduce, the entire genetic line suffers or even goes extinct, and this is the entire soap opera going on in this kind of consensual worlds and realities. But since only the Masses have to go to jail and since the Masses have no choice in this world, everything is part of the continuous eradication. Until it gets to your own social level and it becomes relevant, but by then, you do not have a choice anymore in this world, since you are already on the bottom social level, and this is the kind of soap opera going in the middle social class. While the Elite have a big laugh, enjoying their opulent life at their best, while reproducing accordingly.

Why should a majority always allow an Elite minority to harm this world in this manner, mostly since it had been going on for millennia now, from one elite dynasty to another? This is how the Consensual Matrix prefers it, since the same dynasties span the Consensual Matrix in all its realities. While from local perspectives, once those below learn of this entire consensual social scheme, as underdeveloped as they are, they fight hard to find their own way into the Elite, even by harming or exterminating the rest of their world even more dreadfully. And the cruelest always wins, this cumulative cruelty strengthens the Consensual Matrix, this makes the first, consensual, servitude level so strong and popular, and it happens with everybody. Because this is exactly the underdevelopment taking place at all levels, through all selves of all lifelines of existence, and in all realities.

Note how you can live an entire life subconsciously through needs, feelings, and reflexive behavior, and this defines entirely the second level behavior. Science and psychology push today the idea that humans live their lives entirely through feelings, and they claim this to be the greatest achievement of humanity. They call humans sentient, humans are the only ones to enjoy feelings, and therefore humans are the most intelligent, the most evolved in the universe. I refer to this entire dogma as sentientism, and it shapes society today as it is, since it is pushed on people through all means, as it manages to corrupt everybody today.

Are feelings good or bad? Feelings are certainly good, since they motivate living beings to do everything that they have to do throughout life. Feelings help intelligent human beings to find their place within their inner and outside worlds, helping them maintain cooperation and harmony there. Feelings also allow for the second level thinking, a type of cognitive behavior that is evolved, and this differentiates vertebrates from the rest of the animals. Yet all animals seem intuitive when you study them closely, along with all plants when you study their behavior as an entire species over long periods, since Life is intuitive entirely, and more. However, when as a society, you contort your ideology in order to determine your people to exploit their feelings for selfish meanings and remain disconnected, it interferes with their natural feedback mechanism, causing them to alter their behavior consensually, with the purpose of weakening them and making them less capable, less self-reliant, and more obedient. Therefore, exploiting feelings for selfish, lower level meanings may not be such a good idea, or at least not for human beings, which are the most intelligent living beings in the known universe. Because you keep them down in this manner, at the second level thinking and lower, you keep them disconnected from one another, and so you have the human behavior on Earth as it manifests today, along with all current social problems.

Humans are intuitive at the second developmental level, as they are logical at the first algorithmic developmental level. Yet humans do not think at the second and first levels, but they are capable to think at the third intelligent level, through genuine deductive, inductive, abstract, conceptual, complex, analytical, communicative, intelligent, modeling, creative reasoning. If you fail to develop and if you fail to perform any of these types of third level thinking, you feel it through intense punishment as boredom and depression. And now you have to take drugs in order to manage the punishment resulting from not employing your human reasoning in a comprehensive manner. And this defines the human condition today.

Is science ignorant or concealing, when it comes to understanding and explaining thinking in general, along with the human reasoning in particular? Science may claim anything it wants, as it always does. Yet identical types of errors in scientific reasoning and scientific knowledge appear everywhere, they are very consistent, and they certainly point to ignorance and even to lower levels of thinking.

For example, while attempting to create second level intuitive computer artificial intelligences using computer code, programmers still use algorithms and algorithmic computer models in programming, which are of the first cognitive level, remaining incompatible with second level intuition. Yet algorithmic cognitive behavior will always lead to first level thinking, regardless of the complexity of the program. There are programmers achieving intuitive programs through the same type of repetitive, cyclical, developmental thinking that we have studied in the last chapter, and they stop at this rudimentary second level thinking. It is still an achievement, yet they will never advance, since they do not understand even these results.

We will see in the next chapter how thinking relates to classes of life directly. Because if you want to develop intuitive artificial computer intelligences past the low second level, you have to tap into life and into classes of life, which might be impossible to do using digital technology. Because you need a platform or inner reality of higher informational resolution than what digital platforms and digital realities are capable to offer. Quantum digital computing is still low in resolution, as you need continuous, analogue computing technology to progress throughout the cognitive levels, and it is hard to develop and program it artificially, mostly in a consensual world, with all constraints present.

Yet regardless if intelligences are natural or artificial, if they animate organic life or any other form of life, if they are part of simple or complex classes of life, all intelligences are very similar and they behave very similarly regardless of the species that they happen to animate, and this is the case at each developmental level and at each class of life. Therefore, even you as an intelligent human being may live your life sometimes at lower developmental levels, through intuitive or algorithmic thinking, not because you are incapable or because you are decaying, but because you live your life through your subconscious intelligences directly, while your conscious mind may tend to something else. And as long as you remain aware of your entire cognitive behavior, as long as you understand it well, and as long as you keep it cooperative and harmonious, it is good.

At the third intelligent level thinking, people are careful with their mental models, detailing them excessively in order to have everything taken care of before they even start working on the project for real. People who think at the second level remain unaware of the cognitive structure and procedure of their thinking in general, and of their cognitive behavior in particular. And so they start the real project directly, and then while working, they have to figure out how to solve every problem that they encounter. They experience delays in this manner, and many times, they have to abandon the work and start all over, losing time and materials. Yet everybody does the same, so usually, there is nothing wrong with second level thinking. At the first level thinking, people take only orders from their supervisors, they do what they are told, exactly they are told, they never get in trouble in this manner, and it can never be their fault if everything bad ever happens. Everything is fine at the first level, guaranteed. And this is why the first level is so stable, forming entire consensual matrices spanning the wider world, all compatible with each other, and all forming the Consensual Matrix.

How exactly do you perform your cognitive behavior consciously, at the third, rational level characteristic to living human beings? The third level cognitive behavior involves several other activities and not only mental modeling, including learning, memorization, feelings, perception, logic, and creative abilities. These cognitive activities are part of your reasoning and cognitive behavior, and we have to model them in order to understand them. Yet out of all, mental modeling is the most important human cognitive ability, and in itself, it is the most important activity of your cognitive behavior, since everything from your cognitive lifeline of causality is done with this purpose, to assure your mental modeling. As stated, all intelligences of your cognitive system use mental modeling, and when these are successful, they pop up the results of their mental models in your conscious mind, as successful subconscious ideas, and as needs.

And this is how you have your creativity, ideas, and needs, through other mental models going on in parallel throughout your cognitive system, a multitude of them, all specialized. Or this is how you have them on a subconscious level, because you may conduct your own mental models yourself, consciously. People thinking at the second level may perform even important mental models with their subconscious mind, always waiting eagerly for any idea to pop up in their mind, test it with their feelings, and take credit for it. Under real, objective, and scientific circumstances, you may conduct your mental models consciously, in a normal manner. Yet in art, you have to involve your highconscious to help you with your artistic mental models, or to perform the mental models entirely, otherwise, what you obtain might not be what you want. Because art is the entertainment of the soul, and therefore art must be performed by the soul, for the soul, through a higher level thinking, taking place in your highconscious mind. This is where your artistic creativity comes from, from your higher self, and it is very complex. While you have to interconnect with your highconscious mind in order to have your higher, creative ideas. Yet this is higher behavior and not only cognitive behavior. If you are ever capable to create this necessary higher interconnectivity within your cognitive system.

Why exactly do you have to model everything in your mind before you perform your real, objective behavior? Because it is easier to fail in your mind than to fail in the real world. Many times, it saves you time and money, while other times, it saves your life and the life of those around. You manage to plan and predict everything in this manner, consciously and subconsciously, assuring your success, since mental modeling helps you detect dreadful future consequences of your current behavior.

All living beings reason because this is how and why intelligences always reason, since all living beings are intelligent, and therefore this is how they reason. You can never split apart life, bodies, and intelligences as biology and psychology do, because life, intelligence, and the physical body are correspondences or perspectives of a same oneness, they are your lifeline of existence, and they are always together while defining it.

While through third level mental modeling, you have the chance to memorize your successful ideas, your successful result, the final knowledge that you have found yourself though your modeling, in order to use it at a later time.

However, you do not even have to reason throughout life, because you may always take your ideas from others, in form of readily available knowledge. You find and memorize these from books, testimonies, and from school, and so you have all the knowledge that you need to fulfill your needs, for life. Or this is the task of education, to provide you with all the necessary knowledge to last you a lifetime. You still have to use your advanced reasoning in order to decide what is the best knowledge to use and when, but in time and through experience, you can still manage to think and fulfill your needs, through readily available knowledge.

Besides, this entire readily available successful information is at the first level, structured in first level algorithms, and therefore you may assimilate it and use it through a first level thinking. The problem is that this readily available information applies only within the consensual social environmental matrix, and when you study it closely, it consists of beliefs, since it is dogma. The information still works and you may always use it to fulfill your needs within society, but it works within the Consensual Matrix. While it is the one creating all your developmental problems, causing you to lose control repeatedly and to feel dreadfully bored and depressed, causing you to take drugs continuously, and causing you to drop in development.

What is this Consensual Matrix exactly? You may see its regular pattern through all social hierarchies including the current consensual hierarchic Brotherhood and the Masses. You may feel it through your continuous cognitive discomfort that you have throughout life, and through the continuous fear of those socially above. You may understand it through its entire dogmatic knowledge readily available in society. You may match it through your complete devotion, and it will offer you a designated place in any one of its social hierarchies, while it will care for you and tend to all your needs, for you and for your loved ones. Because if you do what you are told, it will take care of you, rewarding you with a level of lifestyle higher than what is out there among the individual masses. And all that you have to do is do your consensual part and keep it instated, through all the consensual orders that you receive and have to fulfill, and through your excellent conduct and extra work.

Why is it only a Consensual Matrix and not a normal environment? Because all normal environments are natural, part of Life and the wider world, while this Consensual Matrix is not, it is only a consensual mesh, and even more, it functions against Life and against humanity. Why is it not stopped? Because it is powered by humanity, against humanity, and it is maintained in this manner from the outside. And according to higher laws, you do not have to save humanity from harming humanity, since it has its own rights to behave in this manner. And this is the extraordinary funeral march taking humanity to its common grave.

Society allows first level of thinking to all members, and this determines a first level behavior. Yet in society, you still have to think at all levels, since life demands it. While many times, your life becomes so unpredictable and so impossible to manage, that nothing that you try helps. And from what it seems, it does not really matter what kind of thinking, cognitive behavior, and physical behavior you undergo, because society persists to consider only first level thinking and only first level behavior, discarding the rest methodically. And this is why the entire world remains at a lower level, with the same alarming news that you see on TV, the same common plots in movies and books, the same kind of people everywhere around, and the same kind of lower level knowledge everywhere.

While if you happen to write a book at the intelligent human level, it is not only ignored as random text, but it is discarded from the start as though it never existed. And with everything being fake and not being real everywhere, and with this world not even expanding past the lower orbit of Earth in the current human knowledge, then this entire reality might not be as dynamic and as interactive as claimed, but it might have its significant limitations.

Yet people prefer living within societies not because they are incapable to live life on their own, not even because they cannot live in solitude anymore in a world counting in billions now, but because within societies, people manage to share information and successful ideas, and therefore are capable to fulfill a large variety of needs, with certainty. Yet you also find friends, partners, and spouses when there are many people around, but about ideas, once people share these ideas and have them memorized, then there is nothing else for them to think about, and so they may live a safe, certain life within their society, at the first level. Life in society becomes predictable in this manner, not only because people have all the necessary information allowing a casual life, but because their environment is social in nature.

And this is the case not only within human societies, but this is the case with fish living together in schools, this is the case with sheep and cattle living together in herds, and this is the case even with eukaryotes living together in organisms, since they gather to live a more abundant, more secure, and more predictable life together. I refer to these gatherings as classes of life, and they may be of many levels.

All intelligences reason through mental models, and similarly, all intelligences seek to live together, for a more certain, more secure, and more abundant life. This is why intelligences form cognitive systems together. Classes of life are of many levels. You have societies of individuals, while their organisms are composed of cells, while cells are composed of cellular components. As a reference, there are billions of people in society, you have trillions of living cells in your body, as each cell has trillions of living cellular components within. At the same time, you have zillions of intelligences in your cognitive system, and there are zillions of these in the entire society. All living beings and all intelligences stated here are unique, they reason uniquely, and they behave in a unique manner. While our model addresses them, it models them, it models what they are, what they do and why, how they interconnect, and with what results.

Can you behave and reason comprehensively everywhere, in all your realities, through all your selves? You reason in your cognitive system, while you behave physically everywhere else, since your environment is objective in all your realities while you are there. And even in your mind, in your cognitive worlds, your behave cognitively in a real, material, objective manner, since all your intelligences are real living beings in all your mind realities. How does everything happen? You have to understand all your selves, realities, and behavior, taking place through all your selves, in all your realities, comprehensively, since it is always interconnected, forming a single lifeline of causality, matching your comprehensive nature and lifeline of existence, along with your lifeline of reasoning, and along with your lifeline of behavior and fulfillment, all being one, all being you.

6 YOUR CONTINUOUS BEHAVIOR IN ALL YOUR REALITIES

How does your comprehensive lifeline of existence become one? How exactly do you become one with your videogame character when you play your videogame for hours and you forget about yourself and the real world? You certainly have to understand reality, existence, cognition, and behavior in order to understand your comprehensive lifeline of existence, to understand yourself.

How do you memorize and how do you learn everything, from a cognitive perspective? How does the human mind work? You simply perceive, study directly, understand everything, you do so subject by subject, and so you place all the necessary information in your mind. You do not store information in your mind subject by subject individually, but you link everything, you relate everything, since you elaborate it while learning. You learn objective and abstract information, and you use your inner language in order to understand everything before you memorize it. And it might seem incredible now, but after you manage to interconnect and store precisely everything, you end up not exactly with a perfectly detailed library of knowledge with meticulously organized data into books, tables, and catalogues, but you actually end up with an accurate, credible, vivid, perfect inner replica of the real world, all memorized, all stored there in your mind.

Just look briefly around now as you read this sentence, to see how you are capable to access rapidly your own replica of this world in order to match fast and identify everything that you focus your attention on in the outside world, just because your surrounding is in your mind exactly as it is in the outside world, as a replica. Study more carefully your replica of this world as you have another look around now, to see how with each object and subject that you see, there is assigned an entire package of information and feelings about the specific object or subject. It is this replica of this world that you always employ in your reasoning, in order to make your mental models, and as it is, it becomes a stage for your mental models. And this is exactly the meaning for your learning and memories, to provide the stage for your reasoning, for your mental simulations. The more perfect your inner replica of this world is, the more knowledge you have about each element, each object, and each subject, the more you are capable to interconnect and relate everything within, the more successful your reasoning is, and therefore the more successful ideas you have. You apply the solution to your problem in the real world, and then in case that it does not work, you are capable to find out why this is the case, and you fix it. And then you may resume your work.

Sometimes, your idea, solution, or procedure works from the first trial, sometimes you try again, sometimes you have to reason while working in the outside world, and sometimes you start working directly without planning and simulating in advance and it may become more frustrating. But you have to get through, eventually, since you have to plan and mental simulate while you work. And now, you have other people to help you along, you have their experience, and you have additional information found on the Internet.

What is relevant to understand here is that throughout your conscious mental simulations, it is you the conscious intelligence performing the simulation, while your primal subconscious intelligences perform their own mental models, many times at the same time with your own conscious model. And they do so only in their cognitive domain, popping up in your mind needs and entire ideas to guide you through your tasks and through the day, continuously. Therefore, you are never alone throughout your behavior, while you still have to be able to identify and make use consciously of these adjacent needs and requirements, otherwise your intelligences work in vain.

Another relevant remark here is that you, the real living being, are also present in your mind, within your inner replica of this world, as your inner self. You exist there at the very center of your inner replica of this world, and this is how you see this world, from a central perspective. That is who you are, and from your central perspective, that is who you are. You mistake your real self from the real world with your inner self. However, at the third intelligent level, you are aware of your entire inner world and of your entire inner self. And it is important to distinguish between the real world and the inner replica of this world, just because you think through your inner replica of this world, and therefore you assume it to be the real world. Your replica of this world is not perfect at all, and now all imperfections get in your way and stop you from reasoning and from understanding the real world for what it is. Because it is a great difference between all the replicas of this world from the minds of all the people in this world, while people in general assume that everything that they believe and know about this world is true, accurate, and real. While it is not, because this world comes with its zillions of details everywhere and at all time, while you may grasp but a few.

And this is the difference between beliefs and accurate facts, because once accurate facts are present in the real world, beliefs may or may not be present in the real world, while they are always present in your inner replica of this world, as though they are also in the real world. And you never know, because your beliefs may exceed in number and influence your accurate facts. And this is exactly how you end up thinking at lower levels, instead of reasoning at the intelligent human level, through genuine, accurate facts, and through genuine, consciously conducted mental models.

And this is how all problems and disagreements start. Because you, your inner self is different than the real you, and it is different than the image that those around have about you. Some people see you through your behavior, some see you as who you really are, while some see you as you see yourself. While nothing concords. As a reference, just take a pencil and start drawing your surroundings, and that is exactly the accuracy of your inner replica of this world. And some people are more talented at learning and understanding than others, and this makes a big difference in life. And this makes a difference in your family behavior and in your social behavior. You should account for this difference, because otherwise, you waste your time with debates and disagreements, since everybody is always right according to their own replicas of this world, while they always debate the replicas of this world of those around.

Among all elements of your replica of this world, people are the hardest to model, understand, learn, and integrate. Because people and intelligences in general are wider and more diverse than entire worlds and realities, since they are entire worlds and realities, as we keep finding throughout the models of this entire book series. Therefore, your social mental models may be your most tedious reasoning, and probably this is exactly why your worst problems may be social in nature.

Social reasoning and social mental models may constitute most of your cognitive behavior, and I refer to it as your cognitive social behavior. You conduct this kind of cognitive behavior continuously throughout life, and many times, you do not even realize it. And then, when you go to bed at night, you cannot sleep, because these social mental models keep going on in your head by themselves, since they have their own actors. These inner actors are the replicas of those around from the real world, and now these act and behave on their own, in your own replica of this world. And they do so mostly after someone does something bad to you, something wrong, which always happens.

These specific mental models are different, because you may not conduct them through your own conscious intelligence, through your own inner self, but you conduct them through actor intelligences, which are exactly your inner replicas of people, of those around, of those involved in the specific problem that now you have to model. And now, these replicas of people keep reenacting the terrible incident endlessly, and you cannot sleep. Because your entire mind tries to find a solution to your problem, and they keep you awake, only for you to help them with your conscious reasoning. But there is no solution to your problem, since others are always to blame in everything happening to you. You are never the problem yourself, and therefore you cannot solve it, or you do not have to solve it, or this is what you always think, because your own replica of this world is different than theirs.

And so you drink a drink, smoke a smoke, take a pill and kill your intelligences in this manner, since everybody does so. You kill those actors entirely, after you have worked so hard to detail and integrate them perfectly your entire life. Because this is exactly how drugs work, prescribed or not, they kill the neurons holding your intelligences along with the entire knowledge, so your mind becomes dead and empty.

Is this inner replica of this world real? No, not at all, since the real world is out there. Is your character from your videogame real? No, not at all, but it is real only on the display of your laptop, and nothing more. Or it is real, but on that display. While all daydreams that you have are not real at all. Or they are real, but only in your mind world. Which is not real, but only an inner replica of this world, replica where you may reason and simulate anything that you want, even entire films and books if you want, along with everyone in them. And these make up for all your daydreams, reveries, and fantasies, but they are not real, or not exactly real, or not entirely real. Well then, let us study all these.

In order to distinguish what is real from what is not real in this world, you have to understand Existence. Existence has three natures, which are three relative correspondent perspectives. And these are the only perspectives, being relative to your place of reference, the place where you are or where you exist objectively now.

Existence is objective, subjective, and highjective in nature. Everything material and objective around is defined by the objective existence. This entire world is objective in nature. This is the case because you are in it now, and therefore relative to you, this real world is objective, which is the case with everyone else from this world.

The subjective existence consists of everything found in a reality lower than this real objective world. Minds and computers are capable to create inner subjective realities, which are the subjective realities of your dreams and videogames. Nothing there is objectively real, but only subjectively real, as you see it from your own real objective perspective. Dreams, daydreams, imagined people, replicas of people, replicas of this world, along with all the videogame characters, are subjective in nature, or subjectively real. It is the same with all characters from films and books, with all the stories in this world.

And to switch perspectives now, from the perspective of all these subjective characters, this entire real world of ours is highjective in nature from their perspective, as they perceive and understand us from their lower subjective realities. If they ever do. Because you can never perceive anything from one reality to another but only interpret things, in a personalized manner. And this is why your understanding of other realities is personalized in nature and it always relates to you.

This world we live in may be the highest upper reality there exists, including all inner realities possible here, all minds and computer games in this world. And these count in zillions. Science considers this world to be the highest one in existential level. Religion and spirituality claim that there are other realities above this world, higher realities to have created this world just as brains and computer hardware create their minds, computer software, and videogames here in our world.

Which one is true? Are there other realities above this one? You will never be able to find out on your own, unless you are told the truth by the higher beings and higher intelligences of the higher realities. Which is the case if all these exist, even highjectively. We may continue this model now through any of these two assumptions, that this world is the ultimate reality, or that there are other, higher realities above this world. The first assumption is what science claims, while the second assumption agrees with what religion and spirituality state, along with millions of people who had managed to exit this world and then came back to tell the story. Yet let us make our model flexible enough to consider both assumptions in parallel, because one of them has to be true. And we do so just in case that when you die and you wake up elsewhere, you are well prepared. Or you wake up here to do everything all over again. Or you wake up nowhere at all, and nothing matters anymore, in a trivial manner. While there are millions of consistent testimonies in this world, about people accessing higher realities in every manner, or returning to these higher realities as souls, calling these home.

All realities are similar in characteristics and structure, regardless if they are subjective, objective, or highjective. And regardless of the reality that you happen to find yourself in, that world is always objective in nature, as long as you are there. Moreover, realities span to include everything that exists objectively. When you dream, you exist in different realities, which may be lower or higher in existential nature. Yet as long as you are in one of them, then that reality is objective in nature, for you, and it defines your objective existence there. As you may have already noticed, many dream realities span as far as that room you are in, and they last for as long as you keep your dream attention on them. If you exit that room in any manner, if you turn around or if you blink harder, you manage to switch away from that reality to somewhere else, or you wake up altogether. If you ever happen to dream extraordinary dreams where you exist for days and years in a row, then those may be higher realities, while you actually dream them with your higher self or soul. When you dream them through your higher self or soul, this is highjective or higher behavior. You may dream other dreams through the cognitive systems of those that you interconnect with in any manner, and you may distinguish these specific realities through their different colors and details. If you happen to see vivid colors, or very pretty colors that your physical eyes are never capable to display in the real world, then you may have the chance to see this world through someone else's eyes, in their dreams, which are now common with yours.

Higher realities also display vivid colors, along with feelings of a very high essence. You may also dream with your own inner intelligences, you may dream within your own inner replica of this world or within their inner replicas of this world, mostly if these dream worlds seem specialized in food or security. You may also dream common dreams within replicas of this world created by a multitude of people as you, to reenact a new movie that you have just watched. You may also find yourself dreaming within books, videogames, paintings and pictures.

All these are your subjective and highjective behavior, taking place within these dreams. What is important to know, wherever you are in your dreams, you tend to behave identically everywhere, as you do in the real world. Because it is the same behavior, as long as you assume that you are in the real world. You follow the same rules and laws as you do here in society, and you display the same behavior everywhere. However, if you become lucid there in you higher or lower worlds where you dream, then your behavior changes to anything you desire, mostly when you assume that nothing that you do within dreams matters in the real world. While it might actually matter or not.

There are some exceptions, but similarly, all the people from your own replica of this world tend to behave exactly as they do in the real world, and they do the same in all your dreams and projections, as though all their replicas are interconnected. Just you are the same one dreaming everywhere, while behaving similarly everywhere.

Or this is the case if you do not start suspecting that you are in a dream. Many times, you wake up immediately when you start suspecting that you dream, as you become lucid in a dream, since you start involving your conscious reasoning, and that relates to your replica of this world and with this world, waking it up gradually. Yet there are cases when you remain stuck in your dreams even after realizing that you dream. And that is exactly when your dream behavior changes. Because once you know that you are in a dream, you start losing control of everything there, and they harass you in every manner as it happens in horror movies. While they may behave in a horrible manner because they do so throughout horror movies. Then they kill you, if they ever do so, and you finally wake up. Yet many people kill themselves in any manner they desire, in order to wake up, and so they do.

Or you understand everything lucidly, you regain your self-control, you manage to control everything, you remain in your dream, you become capable to switch from one dream scenery to another, from on dream reality to another, lower or higher depending on your skills, while your behavior that you undergo in all these realities is not at all comparable to what you do in society. Just because it does not have to compare, not at all, since you have no restraints in your dreams.

Or this is the case only in theory, or only in very rare occasions. It is called lucid dreaming or astral projection, while all drugs and food additives are meant to make this experience impossible indefinitely. And since it takes millions of people throughout this world working directly or implicitly with food additives to stop your mind interacting with higher worlds, and since it takes additional millions of people to hide the knowledge of higher worlds to you, while taking more people to shadowban all those bringing higher information to you, it means that it is highly important to keep you here in this world.

Whatever the case is, all these are separate realities. And

since you encounter and access them in your dreams, you may still refer to them as your cognitive realities. As long as it is your own brain holding the matrices that form the continuums of all these realities.

All realities are similar in structure, yet all realities are unique in themselves. Realities may come in various densities, sizes, and meanings. Some realities may be artificially created, as computer videogame worlds, while the great majority of created realities are cognitive in nature, as your inner replica of this world where you reason and mental model as an inner self.

Note that there is a difference between the brain and the mind, between the cell and the cellular intelligence, or between the computer hardware and the operating system. Because some are objective, and these form, create, and maintain inner realities. The mind is not the inner reality of the brain, but the mind is the summation of all inner cognitive realities that it represents, as they are held by the brain. Similarly, intelligences exist within realities, many times by the zillions. Simultaneously, intelligences are capable to form inner realities within their own cognitive systems, which form inner realities on their own.

Realities have a similar structure. There is always a continuum, along with the natural laws of that specific reality at the base of everything that exists in that specific reality. In our case, our spacetime continuum and our natural laws of this universe are at the base of everything from our world or universe, containing all elementary particles, all electromagnetic radiation, along with the entire field. Or the field is part of the continuum. Regardless of the case, the continuum, the field, the electromagnetic radiation, and all elementary particles are capable to form everything objective in nature that you see everywhere, by the natural laws of our world. This continuum is the firmament of everything, it is at the base of everything, and it is the very bottom of any reality, as seen from within that reality.

Note that you are never capable to exit any reality by walking to its end, since realities contain everything that exists objectively, containing you, wherever you go. You may not exit realities by going outside the continuum either, even though the continuum is at the base of everything. However, you may always interact with the higher reality that holds the matrix of your current reality, through the continuum and through the matrix holding it, in order to make changes to your world, if you know how. And if you know how, then this is called manifestation, materialization, or direct manifestation, and it can bring you everything. Or this is the case in theory, because when you manifest anything, as objects, subjects, people, and events, you interfere with the overall timeline of that reality, and there are people in this world who own the current timeline just as you own your shoes, interfering now with their property and they are not too happy, so they might not allow it.

Yet this is only a consensual agreement, because as long as you have your ability to change the current human timeline, you may do so as you please. While the Consensual Matrix states otherwise, that timelines and lines of causality in general are property, and must be treated accordingly.

You can never enter other realities directly with your current physical body, and you cannot transfer objects and information from one reality to another. You may transfer only copies of information and replicas of objects and people from one reality to another, and these copies and replicas are always interpretations and not exact copies. You already know about transferring objects, since you cannot take reveries from your mind to make them real, but if you doubt about transferring information, next time when you dream, try to read anything, a book or a sign, a number on a watch, anything at all, and then do so again, to find the words and numbers changed, even as you watch, and you cannot understand anything.

Similarly, you have to learn all information from the real world when you transfer it to your inner replica of this world, where you keep it as memories and understandings of everything from the outside world, in form of concepts and conceptions there in your mind or inner replica of this world.

And this is why you have to know everything in an accurate manner, since it affects the accuracy, pertinence, relevance, and therefore success of your reasoning, further influencing the accuracy, relevance, pertinence, and success of your inner behavior, outer behavior, family behavior, social behavior, and higher behavior. All behavior is correspondent wherever you undergo it, since you undergo it with all selves of your lifeline of existence, as you soul's soul, soul, inner selves from your mind, outer self or physical body, political persona if you have any, and online avatars and videogame characters. And since all these selves are correspondent, then their behavior is correspondent.

All concepts and conceptions from your inner replica of this world are real, objective, material, intelligent, and alive in your inner replica of this world, for as long as you are there, because everything is objective in all realities from your own perspective there, and for as long as you are there. Furthermore, all concepts and conceptions may roam freely in your inner replica of this world, behaving naturally there, but they do so exactly as they do in the outside world, in a correspondent manner. With their life and with their behavior always helping you throughout your reasoning or mental modelling.

As a reference, conception means living being, brought to life there in that specific world of your mind. Because this is how you transfer information from one reality to another, you have to learn and understand it there in your inner replica of this world, and you do so by giving birth to it directly in your inner replica of this world, calling it concept or conception. Which is actually a genuine intelligence of your inner replica of this world, as it is newly specialized in a correspondent manner as it is in the outside world.

It is easier to understand your conceptions of everyone you know in the outside world, since these are alive in the outside world and in the inner replica of this world in a correspondent manner. Yet all your conceptions are similarly alive and correspondent in your inner replica of this world from the perspective of the inner replica of this world, including your concepts or understandings of objects, events, and circumstances of the outside world.

And just as you form your entire inner replica of this world as a conscious intelligence or inner self, similar intelligences form your subconscious mind by the zillions in a specialized manner, in order to be able to tend to the zillions of inner tasks of your organism. While all intelligences and inner worlds and realities of your mind and body are the actual mind and body altogether, the entire organism, one cell after another, the entire physical body.

While it is similar with all living beings and intelligences of the wider world, since they form the entire wider world in this manner, the entire Life, or Intelligence, or wider world, since it is the same. And this is why you find yourself dreaming, reasoning, projecting, and therefore existing and behaving in many worlds and realities, which always seem to be correspondent to this world, since correspondence itself is a supreme law or characteristic of Life.

While you always seem to be unconscious there while still behaving adequately, until you gain lucidity, which is a rare event. And then when you gain lucidity, you tend to wake up. But if you gain lucidity in your dreams or projections, just take your time to study everything in details, as the colors, objects, people, behavior, meaning, and results. And if everything that you read does not maintain consistency when you read it twice, it means that that specific reality is of a lower existential resolution. Or it might mean that you reason within the inner replica from your mind in this world, and not there in the dream world, since there are many circumstances.

Because you are trying to involve your conscious mind while you dream, while it is not capable to transfer conscious information from one reality to another, but only interpretations, and these may change. Channeling is the same, since all channeling represents interpreted information, while that information may be real and accurate in the other reality. Yet some people are better at channeling than others, and there are people in this world capable to show results. And this is the case just because all realities include everything that exists objectively, and if you manage to transfer anything objective or entirely accurate, than it is part of the same reality and you do not channel, but communicate within that reality.

And this is why when you follow a guru, you follow his or her interpretation of the higher reality, which means that you follow beliefs, and not accurate higher knowledge. This is why religion and spirituality are made of beliefs, while these form dogma and ideologies, because you cannot have accurate knowledge transferred from one reality to another, but only interpreted knowledge, and these are called beliefs.

You may not walk to the end to exit realities directly, you may not transfer or fall through the continuum in order to exit or enter realities, but you simply switch to other realities, or you manifest yourself there. And you always do so through your own self, but only when parts of yourself already exist there. Because you happen to be larger and more complex than entire realities, since you exist in many realities even simultaneously, with one of your selves in each one or your worlds and realities. While you also form in yourself countless of these entire realities and clusters of entire realities through your reasoning, even now, as you read this book. And dreams are similar.

We keep our second assumption, that this world is not the ultimate reality, and there are other, higher realities above, forming an entire wider world, by the zillions. Yet if the first assumption is true, that our world is the ultimate reality, as the current science states, then your dreams are simple aberrations and random bioelectric currents animating randomly images, sounds, feelings, and impressions, while flatlines are flatlines, and they always represent death.

And now if you decide to choose one specific assumption because you believe it to be true, you may end up integrating beliefs in your cognitive system, while you should use only accurate facts. Or if someone tells you that a specific assumption is true, then that is still a belief, it is their belief.

You need accurate facts to help you choose one assumption, an accurate experience that you had yourself, an accurate model, an accurate reasoning and understanding. And if so far, you are not convinced by any of the two assumptions, then do not choose any, and keep your reasoning flexible until you know if there are higher realities than this world, or this world is the ultimate reality.

Because if this world is not the ultimate world but only created naturally or artificially within the wider world, then it does not have to be as large as it seems to be, since it is only a correspondence of the higher world where it is made, held, and maintained.

Which means that nothing has to exist past the lower orbit of Earth, not even the Moon, the Sun, and the stars, with all lights that you see in the sky placed there to enhance credibility of a larger world. However, all space objects, along with the entire universe can exist objectively within the higher realities above our world.

Yet there is more to the moon landing, because coincidentally, there are no accurate records taken from the higher orbit of Earth either. If you search the Internet, you find only composite images of Earth taken from space, with everything that is claimed to be accurate showing the oceans of Earth, along with a large amount of cloud formation impossible to form and exist on Earth. There are no accurate records of anything to have gone past the low orbit of Earth. With the moon landing is understandable, because it had humans involved and it was difficult to make that space mission viable, and this was probably the reason to fake it. But it is claimed that there are countless of satellites in the high Earth orbit capable to snap a genuine picture of Earth from space, while you cannot find any reliable genuine material to study, but only fakery. Space missions sent probes throughout the entire solar system as science claims, yet none ever shows accurate pictures and videos, but only irrelevant material, as spikes on a graph. Is this material fake too? For reasons of incapability too? Or everything is a decoy to hide something else, that the entire model for space and the universe that science offers is entirely erroneous, while the initial religious and spiritual models are closer to what is going on out there and up there.

Is Earth real? Is life here on Earth real? Earth does not have to be a hologram in order to be unreal, because this entire world may be a simulation or a model generated by any brain or computer in the higher reality, in any manner and not only as a hologram. Yet this is already our second assumption, and we are already addressing it in this model. Regardless of what this world is as seen from our higher reality, everything is normal and objective as seen from our own world, and therefore it is objectively real, since everything exists in an objective manner in the specific reality that you currently inhabit.

And now, is the Earth flat? Earth may be anything, as long as you know nothing accurate about Earth and this entire world. Science states that Earth is spherical and that there are many stars and galaxies in an entire universe, while some conspiracy theories state that the Earth is actually flat and the Elite hide the truth about Earth. Yet by the way everybody behaves at all social levels, it seems that everybody is ignorant, cannot reason, and do not know the truth. With all Brothers proud the entire time of their flawless consensual behavior hiding the accurate truth, which they never actually know themselves, but they are still proud of hiding it.

There are many theories and ideologies constraining the people to assume various knowledge, and this is what everybody does. Since in a consensual world, you never seek the truth, but you follow orders and assignments, in order not to get in trouble. While you still get in trouble and they take you out, and now this is this world, flat or spherical.

How exactly do you dream, and how do you transfer yourself into dreams at night? You dream with your dream body. Yet it is more likely that you dream within your own mind, or within the minds of other people that you know. Or you might dream throughout the higher worlds, depending on circumstances.

Yet you always need a body in the other reality where you dream, an avatar, in order for you to exist in that reality while you dream. And you do so shortly, before switching to other realities. While other people pop up near you wherever you dream, and then when you switch to other dream realities, they still follow you, popping up the entire time. Which is the case with toddlers and pets, even in large numbers. While they have their friends and family members with them since these follow them around, or not, since there are many cases.

Similarly, many religious characters are considered avatars of the Divine himself or not, since religions count in tens of thousands believing everything. While you have to play your videogames through your characters, which become your avatars there in the computer videogame world. The word 'avatar' is thousands of years old or probably more, and in its own, this tells you something about this world.

It is relevant to know how you get there, in the other realities, even through your avatars. You project there, but you do not go there, and you do not appear there. You project in a new medium, which is capable to hold your new intelligence. 'Projection' does not mean jumping into something, as jumping in a pool, or a projectile projecting anywhere, but it is more as the projection of an image onto something, as in a mirror. Because when you project in a mirror, there are two images, since there is your image from the real world, and then there is your projection in the mirror that you may also see. There are two images of you, in two different mediums. Only that through consciousness projection, you do not project images, since these are still objective in nature and therefore part of the objective world, but you project your current consciousness into another medium, which is capable to hold another reality, which is capable to hold intelligences, and there, as one of these intelligences, you project.

What you do, you switch your consciousness from this real body to the body of that intelligence from that other medium where you project. From the perspective of this world, you may refer to all living beings of other realities as spirits or intelligences. Yet from the perspective of those realities, all these spirits have normal bodies, are alive, living a normal life there. Therefore, when you project, you switch consciousness from this real body to a specific body from that reality. Or if you are very skilled, you do not need a new body at all, but only an imaginary point of reference. Yet it also depends on the reality where you project.

For example, here in this world, your real body is not you the conscious intelligence. This conscious intelligence lives throughout the body but it can project in your prefrontal cortex as your intelligent inner self, and you may see it lighting up on an EEG display when you think of anything consciously. This conscious intelligence also assumes to be the real body from the outside world when it projects once again in the physical body of the outside world, just because all senses of perception are placed on the physical body in this world, at its own level.

Yet there are more of you on your lifeline of existence, since you are all your higher selves or souls from your higher worlds, plus all your inner selves from your mind including your conscious intelligence and your intelligent inner self from the cortex, plus your outer self or the physical body here in this world, plus your videogame characters, political persona, and theatrical persona if you are an actor.

And you always project one in another in another in another, until you project in your intelligent inner self from the intelligent inner replica of this world from the cortex where you reason, daydream, and mental model. And then as the intelligent inner self, you may access your senses of perception and your muscles to project once again, in your entire physical body, to exist in this world, where you may interact with this world in any manner while fulfilling your needs and meanings.

While the entire time you may be only your conscious intelligence behaving the entire time on your own, or you may be any one of your souls behaving on its own the entire time as the conscious intelligence and then as the inner selves, and then as the physical body.

Yet souls my do so or not, since souls also live their own higher lives in their own higher worlds, apart from you in your mind or here in this world. With some souls becoming more or less involved in this world. While being mostly interested in drugs, violence, specific important life events, fashion, career, animal fulfillment, family life, material achievements, spiritual achievements, religious achievements, brotherhood achievements, learning, and teaching.

Since I noticed higher selves and higher beings in general developed at all possible levels, while behaving in all possible manners. While among everything interesting them in this world, are drugs. And the thrilling, unusual experiences. Been there done that. Along with the chance to be and experience life as various characters of this world. Or the chance to be with their higher loved ones in this world for an entire lifetime, or the achievement itself of make it throughout an entire life here, or the achievement to learn various knowledge and become involved in various experiences. While other higher beings live here in this world life after life after life, while calling this world their world, since this is where they live continuously, not in their higher world. Similarly, some people play videogames online continuously, and there is where they actually live.

You the conscious intelligence do not really project into your replica of this world, but into your intelligent inner self from your inner replica of this world. You assume your physical image and physical body to be your intelligent inner self from your inner replica of this world. You are capable to control it directly and consciously in this manner, as you please. If you never did so, then your inner self from the replica of this world functioned and acted normally and independently, as all replicas of real people from your inner replica of this world.

This is why, whenever you severe this direct cognitive link with your inner self, then you experience in the real world a condition called total amnesia. You still function in the real world, but as an entirely new human being, having forgotten all personal information. It is another group of neurons close by, becoming your intelligent inner self now. And it is him or her now living your life consciously, living its own life as himself in the mind and in the outside world, if it is capable enough to reconstruct all neural interconnections to all conscious cognitive activities managed by the previous intelligent inner self.

You also have replicas of other people in your inner replica of this world, and these are genuine projections of the real people from the outside world. When the real people from the outside world, as your loved ones, manage to interconnect with their counterparts from your inner replica of this world, then they also manage to interconnect with you as in the example with Rebecca. And you become who you are, the living nature, and not some simple social information about yourself. And at night, you may project into each other's replicas of this world through your counterparts, to have common dreams, which is a common experience. You were supposed to be able to project at any time in this manner, even during the day and even during conscious activity, and this is called astral projection. Or you could go together to other worlds.

Witches, angels, and shamans are simple examples here. These other realities are called shems, while the word shaman means inhabitant of an astral world, or wonderer through an astral world. And this was a very common experience before the drugs, food additives, vaccines, and before the forbidding ideologies took everything away.

This is your higher behavior, since you perform it through a higher ability. This used to be a normal behavior of the third level, yet humans live life disabled cognitively, with their highconscious many times entirely amputated. And this is why I do not consider highconscious abilities to be part of the third level abilities, but part of the fourth level. Again, what affects your highconscious intelligence today are additives in everything, medication, vaccines, stereotypes, ignorance, false science, continuous obedience, lack of specific nutrients, lack of knowledge, ideologies, taboo, and lack of higher development, all determining and maintaining instated the Consensual Matrix.

You do it to yourself. While as you notice lately, the Consensual Matrix targets you directly as a Brother, taking away your higher existence and higher nature systematically, while exploiting you even more. Because after you finished the Masses, now it is your turn.

The replicas of the people that you know live right now within your own replica of this world, regardless if they are interconnected or not with the real people outside. Similarly, within their replicas of this world, you live your life normally, and you participate in all social mental models whenever the time comes for you to play your part in that specific model throughout reasoning, and so you predict your future behavior from there, from the mind of those around. These replicas of yourself from the mind of those around may be interconnected or not with your inner self, depending on these intelligences, since every one of these replicas is an intelligence. While many times, intelligences interconnect or become one when they have many characteristics or abilities in common. Because intelligences are not as distinct in a continuum as individual living beings are, but intelligences are only projections within bodies of living beings, projections of a one intelligence, in bodies that may be human or not, organic in form or not.

As a reference, your brain is your current medium, and it is capable to hold all your intelligences, including your conscious intelligence. And since you still assume that your own inner self is the real you, you also assume that your own inner self is your conscious intelligence. Which is not too bad, since others may assume that you are only your behavior, only your identity information, or only your physical body.

How do you enter your dreams, through your inner self, or through your conscious intelligence? Yet you do not get there through these, but you get there through their projections. Because other mediums are capable to form separate realities, and you may not go from one reality to another. You may not go from one brain to another. And this is why you have to have your own self in these different mediums first, and then you have to interconnect with them, as in the example with Rebecca. However you dream or project there, and whenever you do so, you have to lose consciousness and change selves and therefore consciousness first, since consciousness is different for each self and reality. And this is how you may end up with a separate self and a separate consciousness for each reality where you dream or project. It seems tedious or chaotic, but there is order in this model.

How do you create a new intelligence in a new medium in order to interconnect with it and project there, at night or whenever you want? You do so through your higher self. If not, you do so through another self. Or if not, other intelligences native to that specific medium do so for you.

As a reference, it is you the conscious intelligence to have learned and assimilated knowledge throughout life constructing this inner replica of this world from your own mind. What you did your entire life, you projected diligently everything from the outside world, everything that you perceived, everything that you found relevant, and everything that you could understand, you projected everything in a new medium, in your own brain, in your mind, which is a lower reality in itself, and you projected everything there in form of your entire inner replica of this world. Your inner replica of this world consists of all objects from the outside world, all subjects and all knowledge, and more importantly, it consists of all people from the outside world that you have encountered long enough for them to become relevant to your life and to be part now of your inner world.

Now others project in your own mind, through their own inner selves that you have replicated in your own mind. And through a total interconnection, the real and the replica become one. Everything becomes more important when after death, these real and replicated intelligences still remain interconnected with their counterparts, making for a special, yet common interconnective behavior. Just do not tell anyone, since you end up with medicine.

And if these specific replicas of people that you have within your own replica of this world happen to behave now freely throughout your mental models, daydreams, and dreams, everything is real. Everything is real for them, they simply live their own life there, within your own inner replica of this world, while they remain unaware of the real world, and of the fact that they are only a replica. Right now, as you read, they certainly found out, while they still help you reason, interpret, distinguish knowledge, and assimilate it within your comprehensive replica of this world.

This does not mean that they believe it entirely to be true, since you do not believe it either entirely to be true. And you always share your cognitive feelings with all intelligences of your cognitive system, everything being part of your second level intuitive thinking. Yet you keep your replica of this world flexible, and in the future, if any of these makes sense, then it becomes an accurate fact. Or if any of your main, trusted characters of your inner replica of this world find this to be true, then you tend to consider it true. Or if some or most of the knowledge of this book helped you understand many topics that you could not understand before, then you tend to consider the rest true.

Because when you have misunderstandings within your inner replica of this world, everything seems crooked and incomplete there. And many times, this is why you search everywhere for specific knowledge, because you receive your human needs for learning and for cognitive maintenance, and you do so in order for you to complete your remaining, missing knowledge, or to repair what does not make sense. And if you complete your replica of this world now in many instances, then you certainly seek to complete the rest. And what it is accomplished in this manner, you certainly believe to be true, because it is very true in the general context of your entire replica of this world. You are also rewarded for these cognitive accomplishments, with happiness and completion through serotonin.

Furthermore, if any of your authorities validates this knowledge, then it becomes an accurate belief by default. Because people still listen to their designated informative authorities, as the evening news, presidents, and teachers at school. Or if this information happens to be useful in developing your higher abilities, and if through them you find out that this knowledge is true, then you certainly believe it to be accurate.

But is it an accurate higher belief, or an accurate higher knowledge? Yet you believe everything to be true, not entirely, but only partially, while you already knew most or some of what you find here, as you already suspected part of it to be true.

What is the difference between knowledge, beliefs, higher knowledge, higher beliefs, accurate beliefs, and accurate knowledge? Higher knowledge is knowledge coming from the higher world, it comes through your higher self or your highconscious mind, and it may be interpreted and not exactly true. Beliefs are only considered as accurate knowledge, for various reasons, as a form of ignorance, or as a form of dogma, or social stereotypes. Higher beliefs are as higher knowledge, only coming in form of beliefs from the higher world. And they come in this manner because there, in the higher world, they are not knowledge, but beliefs. Accurate knowledge relates to the natural facts of the universe, which are the natural facts of this world. They are knowledge relating directly to our spacetime continuum, to the field, to all particles and radiation, and to all natural, physical laws keeping these entrained throughout time and space. These accurate facts or accurate knowledge are the accurate mathematics, which is most of mathematics, they are accurate physics, which is the classical physics: mechanics, thermodynamics, and optics, along with the accurate part of electrodynamics including Maxwell's Equations, and more.

As you notice from all models of this entire book series, it is possible to use these accurate facts and mental model to understand biology, psychology, sociology, and economics. As a reference now to our task of finding which one of the two assumptions is true, is this world the ultimate reality, or only an ordinary reality and part of the wider world, you have to take your judgment all the way down to these natural facts of the universe, down to the classical mechanics and mathematics, in order to find which assumption is correct. Yet in this manner, you obtain only an accurate fact here in this world, but not higher knowledge. While you might need higher accurate knowledge to find out the truth about the higher nature of our world and of all living human beings.

And this is how you distinguish the good from the bad in this world, as you do so through all cognitive means. This is how you distinguish facts from beliefs, along with what is real from what is fake. And then once you do, once you learn to reason for yourself, all your ideologies, if you have any, ridicule, marginalize, punish, and banish you, because they cannot tell you anymore what is good and what is bad in this world, they cannot mislead you anymore, and therefore they cannot control you anymore. And this makes the difference between controlled behavior and free behavior. And if you decide right now to transit from a controlled behavior to a free behavior, expect a large amount of endurance on the way.

What is relevant to understand here is the fact that if for you, these mental models are subjective in nature, from the perspective of your intelligences within your replica of this world, everything there is objectively real, since that is their objective reality. Their entire world is real and objective for them, just as you have created it there as an intelligent inner self. And this is exactly how your reasoning takes place, through these subjective mental simulations from your own perspective, which are also objective in nature from the perspective of all intelligences inhabiting your inner world, which is what they consider to be their real, objective, material, normal world.

Yet their world is not as stable as this world, but it changes, in order to match your reasoning, becoming the multitude of separate settings that you have to consider throughout your reasoning. While the intelligences enacting your relevant circumstances are always the same ones, probably not even realizing that you switch them continuously from one instant or setting of your inner world to another throughout your reasoning. In theory, they reason for you while you do not do much, or while you do not even notice, but you only accept and consider the result, whatever result they found by the end of their entire event.

And probably this is why this world cannot be complete in all instances and in all details, because this world does not have to be real entirely, but only as much and as long as it is necessary for its cognitive meaning to be achieved, with the rest being true and real in principle. Because it might be only a scenery and not a world, a simulation of future events done on behalf of the higher world. This is as far as this enacting takes us now, up to the lower orbit of Earth, since existence may stop there and nothing exists beyond. And this is as long as this enacting lasts, until sometimes in the future, when another enacting starts, and we all have to be ready, because we have to live another significant lifetime then, since we have to find another significant cognitive solution for the higher world.

Well, but this is another assumption, because this world does not have to be a reasoning cognitive reality as seen and undergone from the higher world, but it may be a higher daydream, a common reverie, or a memory of a distant, very distant higher thought, still existing now, as an old, forgotten toy in someone's attic. This world may be a thought or a feeling, it may be love itself or someone's dream at night, it may be your own dream and you are probably on your way to wake up, or it may be an extraordinary computer game, a coma, or a nightmare, since everything is possible. And it is very hard to figure out what it is, without accurate higher knowledge.

Why are we investing this much effort on realities, and particularly on this world? Because minds are realities in themselves. Intelligences behave objectively and cognitively within realities, and therefore your behavior is influenced entirely by all these realities, higher, objective, and subjective. However, there is another reason, and we have to clarify it now. This entire objective world in itself is the cognitive or objective behavior of a higher being, or of a group of higher beings while undergoing it together. And we have millions of testimonies of people to have exited this world, found out the truth, then came back to share the knowledge. And it is a common reverie, done by a multitude of higher beings interconnected cognitively directly within a common inner replica of their higher world. And this specific common inner replica of their world is this entire world, while all their counterparts from this replica of the higher world are them, here. These are the souls. And they are you, because you certainly choose to imagine everything together, and you imagine everything to be exactly it is today, with this specific society and with eight billion people exactly as they are, not better and not worse, but exactly as they are. You certainly did so for a reason, and now this is your behavior, your cognitive and objective behavior at once. This is it, and this higher behavior determines directly your behavior now as you undergo it in society, in the real world.

And if you cannot control it anymore, then there is a higher reason for this, and there might be a higher reason for you to find your way through, to find out how to control your behavior, how to live your life, how to better your life, how to develop, and how to better yourself. Because through you, your higher counterparts or souls better themselves, and they develop with you, alongside you.

So this is your behavior, higher and lower, this is your environment, here on Earth now, these are your identities, higher and lower, and this is this world, according to millions of witnesses. And this is still not an accurate fact, but a very common belief.

We consider millions of testimonies, and therefore why can it not be an accurate fact? Because as stated previously, we have detached from the official validation of everything that is considered true in this world today, because these authorities define the current human knowledge on their own behalf, through consensus, at the first consensual level. Instead, we have decided to rely directly on the natural and supreme laws and facts of the universe, including all concepts and laws of mathematics and classical physics. While all these can assure us the accurate validity of all objective knowledge and of most of subjective knowledge, which is everything related to this world, while this world is and means everything that exists objectively for us. And since the laws of all subjective realities held in our world, the mind and computer worlds, are defined here in this world, we may define accurately implicitly everything from all inner worlds, in theory.

However, you cannot do the same for the higher realities and for the One as a whole, because we cannot know accurately the higher laws defining the One at its tenth supreme existential level. Since in order to do so, we have to be tenth level supreme beings, we have to have a tenth level cognition, we have to have a higher self at the tenth supreme developmental level, and we have to know all tenth level supreme knowledge.

Could we still know everything about our higher reality accurately? It is similar for our higher reality, since we need a fourth level awareness through a higher self or soul capable to reason at the genuine fourth level, by using meaningful, higher, fourth level knowledge. We may still know everything related to our higher world and all its higher beings or souls, yet we do so not accurately but implicitly, through first reference testimonies coming from religious and spiritual characters or from regular people. And even if you learn all higher knowledge yourself, through hallucinogens, astral projection, and NDE, it remains only a testimony for the rest of this world.

You already understand reasoning at all levels, you understand perception and memorization, you understand needs and feelings, and you are ready to understand thoughts. These are part of your cognitive behavior. There is a difference between thoughts and reasoning. Ideas and solutions are thoughts, and you obtain these through reasoning. Knowledge comes in form of thoughts, along with information in general. Yet not all thoughts become successful ideas or important knowledge. Because thoughts are simple changes in your replica of this world, taking place throughout normal eventful life there, throughout your reasoning, and throughout your mental models. Thoughts are outcomes, effects, and achievements within your replica of this world, as these may be concepts and conceptions, which are always intelligences themselves.

Time is also different within your inner replica of this world. What for your inner intelligences of your replica of this world may take an hour, a day, a year, or a lifetime, for you it may take no time at all if you do not pay attention, or it may slow down to take as long as you need, in order to allow you to maintain your attention on them. And now, it may seem that you see your entire replica of this world in your mind from above, as in the "Simcity" videogame, but it is not so. Since your perspective is always within the inner replica of this world, because you always maintain your perspective there, matching it to the one that you have in real life. Characters of your replica of this world are not little people either, running around there, but they are as large as in the real world, and as vivid and as spontaneous as in the real world. It is hard to see your replica of this world during the day while you reason, but at night, you may dream sometimes within your inner replica of this world, and it is just as the real world. While the setting always changes, taking you by surprise many times, because there always seems to be something going on. And you may control these events consciously or not, since everything depends.

These also happens with you from one dream to another, while you never realize that your setting had changed in the dream, but you only behave normally and accordingly wherever you are, for as long as you have to be there.

We may observe here an interconnectivity between all projections found in all replicas of this world acquiring them.

And this specific interconnectivity allows this living being to exist interconnectively in all these separate projections, and through all these separate projections simultaneously, as one.

And this is how you may interconnect with these people yourself, through these replicas or projections within your replica of this world, and through your projection in theirs. And it might seem amusing, but when you dream and you happen to switch from one dream to another randomly or not, your children will follow you around everywhere, popping up in your new setting shortly after you get there, integrating perfectly in the entire environment. Other friends of yours get there, and so you start a party, until you leave to go elsewhere. Your children may leave shortly after, to go to school, or to go to the mall, or to do their homework. They will spend a large amount of time at school with everyone happening to be there, as you dream.

But this is only one type of interconnectivity, because there are many types of interconnectivity in the wider world. Did all these happen with you or with your higher self? With both, because you are one lifeline of interconnectivity. Yet many times, you will dream as someone else, since there are many worlds up there, similar or not to our world.

In what it concerns reasoning now, we notice how all replicas of the real people from the outside world live their lives normally in your mind, at any rate, since time is different there. And now, all their achievements throughout life become your priceless ideas. It is not really you reasoning after all, but them.

There is more to consider, because in all your memories from your inner replica of the word, every house, car, animal, people, are living intelligences, regardless if they are memories of abstract knowledge or of real people, pets, chairs, or cars. They are real intelligences, static or independent.

And this is the case because everything is an intelligence everywhere, while forming an intelligent living being. Spirituality and native people call these intelligences spirits, while I refer to them as intelligences. Intelligences are alive and certainly conscious and intelligent. They are part of the continuum, they are also part of the field from this world, as the electric, magnetic, and gravitational field, while they are also part of the universal field, which is the same field found in all realities, higher and lower, spanning the continuum of the One or wider world.

Our world is held by a higher body similar to a brain or computer hardware found in the higher world, which forms a matrix that is similar to neural impulses or computer language. This matrix, through its intelligent encoding, forms the continuum of that specific inner reality, which is capable to hold everything in that reality.

Note how it is the field from our higher reality forming the matrix holding our world, and further on, this matrix forms the spacetime continuum of our world, while also becoming the field in our world. We notice how it is the field transcending from one reality to another through all matrices, and forming everything in all realities, lower and higher. I refer to this universal field as the field or Universal Mind, since it is the field holding all intelligences in all realities. Intelligences also project from one reality to another along their own lifelines of existence. And this is exactly why I always state that intelligences, along with the living beings that they animate, are more complex, larger, and more capable than entire worlds and realities.

Are intelligences living beings? Yes, as seen from all higher perspectives, since from higher perspectives, all living beings are intelligences. Yet when you study life and living beings from the supreme perspective of Life, Intelligence, and the wider world, all living beings in the wider world become intelligences, since you are at a perspective higher than all of them.

An important detail about intelligences is that they become entire worlds while they reason, by opening new lower realities within their cognitive systems, inner realities capable to hold primal intelligences, along with all inner replicas of this world, along with all intelligences. As seen, intelligences live normally throughout realities, just as individuals live normally throughout societies. Yet all individuals are intelligences in themselves, they are the same. This means that intelligences are in themselves societies of inner intelligences. All these inner intelligences are abilities or specialized intelligences as seen from an upper perspective, while all these abilities or specializations are individual intelligences in themselves, as seen from an inner perspective.

It is the same within any cognitive system, and it is the same within all societies. This is how your primal eating and digestive ability is the primal eating intelligence from its own perspective, while it is the eating ability from the outer perspective of your entire subconscious intelligence. Your eating intelligence has its own abilities, as digestive abilities, food management abilities, and food transportation abilities. Each one of these abilities is an inner intelligence in itself. When you study these abilities, you find them formed of their inner abilities. Therefore, intelligences are never elemental, but they are societies of societies, of societies.

While your intelligent inner replica of this world resides, exists, or lives throughout the cortex, your subconscious covers the entire brain and body, minus the little area in the left prefrontal lobe holding you, the intelligent inner self. As a comparison, your primal subconscious intelligences tend to all the important tasks in your body. Your primal subconscious intelligences also spread out to cover your body, since your entire body is part of your cognitive system.

Compared to your primal intelligences, the memories of your replica of this world are mostly static in nature, each one being kept as wild animals in cages at the zoo, in their intact form, for a sustained accuracy. Only replicas of people are allowed to roam freely as they do in the real world.

Your needs for learning determine you continuously to tend to your inner replica of this world, to consolidate it, to add knowledge to it, and to keep it updated and synchronized with the real world. You are also rewarded and punished for this entire learning process, and you do feel miserable, frustrated, and even depressed, for each inconsistency within your replica of this world. And then, when you learn something very important, or when you manage to finish restructuring important comprehensions of the outside world, you are rewarded greatly, with happiness and peaceful feelings.

All intelligences of your inner replica of this world are different than the primal intelligences of your cognitive system. You the conscious intelligence are very similar to these primal subconscious intelligences, since you are a primal intelligence yourself, the primal conscious intelligence, responsible with the interaction of your entire organism in the outside world, which is your physical or social behavior. You are also responsible with your online behavior, since your online behavior allows you to fulfill some of your needs even when you consider it as simple entertainment. Regardless of what you do, you fulfill your needs throughout life, and therefore you conduct your behavior consciously and you do anything in order to achieve your meaning. And in order to do so, you have to find out how to fulfill your needs, mostly when the environment changes in any manner. Your primal subconscious intelligences send you your needs guiding you throughout your task, and many times, your primal subconscious intelligences fulfill these needs on their own in the outside world for as long as they know how, which is, for as long as the environment remains unchanged.

This is your unconscious behavior, the activity done by your other primal intelligences while fulfilling needs, as riding the bike, putting on shoes, or locking the door. And then, when you go back to check, everything is fine, the door is locked, and the faucet is closed. Because it was not you the conscious intelligence doing these tasks, but your primal subconscious intelligences did, while you forgot to monitor them. Your higher intelligence also becomes involved many times, while you may mistake it with your subconscious intelligence.

Why can't your primal intelligences fulfill their needs by themselves and you have to do so in their place? Because you are more capable and smarter at finding solutions in the outside world. And this is your task, as it is part of your responsibilities, since all goods and all supplies that you have to acquire, and all social tasks that you have to tend to, everything takes place in the outside world.

Why can they not be responsible with the outside world? In fact, less evolved animals may live an entire life unconsciously, through their primal intelligences. If they have any, because if they are not evolved at all, as they live life through their cellular intelligences. As a reference, your cellular intelligences send their needs to your primal intelligences, your primal intelligences fulfill them almost entirely, and what they cannot do, they pass on to the other intelligences by specialization. And to you, the conscious intelligence, since it is a characteristic of human beings to have a very capable conscious intelligence. But to answer the question, your reasoning, your mental models, and your inner replica of this world are capable to tend to the most difficult tasks of the entire organism, and this is what you do throughout life. And if there are tasks that you cannot fulfill, these are your limitations now. However it happens, you have your own replica of this world, while your primal intelligences have theirs, in a highly specialized form. Since in general, all intelligences of the wider world create their own replicas of their environment within the specific medium where they live, and they live there as a conscious intelligence, reasoning through similar mental models as you do, continuously.

You have the brain, which is a physical, objective medium. You have the mind, which contains the inner realities facilitated by the physical medium, and then you have all intelligences inhabiting this mind, this cognitive system, all being specialized, all engaged in a similar reasoning and behavior, which are specialized in whatever they do. They form their own realities containing their own inner replicas of their world, meant to carry their abilities, which are their inner intelligences, which also open inner realities throughout thinking, in order to make mental models and predict outcomes.

Note that minds function through all their cognitive abilities: needs, feelings, reasoning, mental models, reveries, inference, deductive reasoning, intuition, and intelligence. If our world is naturally created, then it is part of these cognitive activities, facilitating any one of them, as a daydream or conscious mental model, as we have already seen. However, if this world is artificially created, by using higher technology as higher computers, then it is still part of the One, as any naturally created reality, simply because it is used by higher beings or souls to fulfill natural needs. Even our Internet is used to fulfill a diversity of natural needs today, and once the brain-computer interface is introduced in society, then the Internet will be able to facilitate the fulfillment of all needs, making possible to live life entirely virtually, through lower realities. And we already see a vertical lifeline behavior here, which is a continuation of the fulfillment of all higher needs through our world, and then further down through our future virtual realities of the Internet, which in themselves are our inner realities.

Regardless if this world is naturally created or artificially created, regardless if it is co-created by a group of higher beings or if it is created by one individual higher being, it still integrates in the wider world and in Life, directly or implicitly, since it can host the living beings of the wider world, and these make it part of Life and the wider world. It is similar with the Consensual Matrix, since despite of what it claims that it stands apart from Life and the wider world, once it interacts with the living beings of Life and the wider world, it interferes with these and therefore it becomes part of them, part of Life and the wider world.

And this is how the wider world turns. And if this world is not the ultimate reality, then it has a cognitive nature, and it is one among zillions of similar realities carrying intelligences that live their normal life, while caught within mental models meant to allow conscious reasoning, or direct feelings, or common daydreams, whatever their higher intelligences demand. And this goes on all the way up to Life herself, and now this is how the wider world turns.

About perception now, you are not the only intelligence capable to access the five senses of perception and remain interconnected with them continuously, since your primal intelligences may do the same. You may all perceive the outside world in this manner, always watching it many times continuously, just waiting for relevant events demanding your activity and involvement. Your security primal intelligence watches continuously for threats, as spiders and snakes, along with sharp objects and threatening individuals, anything that may harm you. And now, when it sees a spider, it takes control of the body, and it induces an innate reflex and it makes you jump, many times unknowingly and unwillingly. Similarly, through your primal intelligences, your subconscious does all subconscious tasks, it watches for food in the outside world, for reproductive partners, for good friends and good company, and for pertinent, proper learning material. And it does so continuously, watching through all its abilities, as security, eating, reproductive, social, and learning developmental.

From your perspective and from the perspective of your subconscious mind, these are distinct abilities. Your subconscious watches this world with them, reasons with them, behaves cognitively and subconsciously with them, and then it sends you relevant needs with these abilities. While from an inner perspective, these abilities are distinct specialized intelligences in themselves, together forming the subconscious intelligence. And with you the conscious intelligence at their side, together forming your cognitive system.

I refer to these subconscious intelligences to be primal, because they do not die with the organism, but they transfer themselves as colonies of intelligences to the next generation at the moment of conception. And they do so from one generation to another, indefinitely. These primal intelligences have been around for billions of years or more, they are highly pertinent, and through their presence, they confirm that they have always been successful at all their tasks, as they never failed, or you were not here to confirm it. This is also your case, the conscious intelligence, since you have always been capable to fulfill all your needs, for billions of years.

As intelligences of a same cognitive system, all your primal intelligences are conscious in what they do, since consciousness and identity characterize all intelligences of the wider world, and there are countless of them out there. They have a similar task, to help their entire objective body to interact with their environment. And they behave in a similar cognitive manner, by creating inner realities, where they perform mental models to find successful solutions by using inner specialized intelligences that open even lower realities in order to reason by creating inner inner realities populated by inner inner intelligences. Through inner replicas of this world, all primal intelligences of a same cognitive system break apart the outside environment or outside world by specializations or by interests, they create inner replicas of this world in their specialization, and that is what they use now to inhabit and reason, without realizing that there is more to this world besides their specialization.

Your primal eating intelligence lives in an inner replica of this world different than yours, just because it performs different tasks throughout the organisms, and therefore it has a different specialized inner replica of its world. Your eating primal intelligence may live in an inner replica of this world resembling to a kitchen, a stove, or a refrigerator, and more. There must be refrigerators and kitchens there, your kitchen and refrigerator, but in the inner replica of this world of your primal eating intelligence there is your stomach, continuously digesting food, and that replica of your stomach exists there in a very precise detail, as precise as the scale of individual cells and lower. Since your primal eating intelligence is responsible with all digestion taking place everywhere, and with all related cellular activity, while receiving feeding needs from all the cells of the body counting in trillions. That is the specialized part of the outside world that your primal eating intelligence interacts with throughout life as a conscious intelligence, and therefore that part of this world is what it replicates now within its own inner replica of this world, only the food sources from the outside world, along with the entire digestive system, along with part of the endocrine system, along with all cells, along with your senses of perception.

In fact, your primal eating intelligence knows exactly where each one of its essential and non-essential nutrients are found in any food product from your refrigerator and cupboards, from any restaurant you go to, and from any shelf of your grocery stores, in what quantity and of what quality. Your eating primal intelligence knows everything, and it makes you eat that specific food when it needs those nutrients. And if you refuse, the nagging never ceases, and you have to give in and you eat that food.

Or this is the case when you do not stand ahead of this nagging to be prepared with proper food that you eat in perfect amounts with each meal, because if you are not prepared, you will waste your time fulfilling one need after another all day long, and you have no time left for your higher needs. Because what you should do, you should eat only two or three times a day, main meals comprising all essential nutrients, along with enough calories to last you until the next main meal. Do not eat between meals, in order not to waste time. Be sure that you know what you eat, and your eating intelligence will never nag again between meals, because you eat everything it needs, daily.

Yet there is more to consider, since as you notice while reading this book, your primal eating intelligence never bothers you right now to go eat, because it allows you to read this book, since it considers it more important. Because your entire subconscious main intelligence keeps you within third level developmental modes of life right now, in order to allow you to learn and develop, with keeping all your primal subconscious intelligences less prioritized, allowing you to read.

While all human beings were supposed to live life only within third level intelligent modes of life, as they learned, developed, and tended to the entire third level intelligent human environment through the fulfillment of their own third level intelligent human meanings in society and in this world. But instead, while underdeveloped, you have all these primal intelligences prioritized, sending you their own needs continuously, as it is the case with all animals. Since this is how you end up eating continuously throughout the day, socializing continuously, or reproducing continuously without actually having children.

While on even lower developmental levels, you serve continuously throughout life, or you take drugs continuously. But if you had the third level human environment all around, it kept you by default at the third intelligent human level, and you never decayed in development throughout the day and throughout life. And now, you, your family, your genetic line, and the entire humankind never died.

And it is the same with all your primal intelligences. You may imagine how the inner replica of this world of your primal reproductive intelligence looks like, how it lives there, what it does there, and what all the replicas of the people from the outside world do there. Yet that may be only part of it, since your primal reproductive intelligence has a wider behavior, including conception, gestation, birth, raising children, educating them, getting them initiated in everything, and teaching them how to tend to all their needs and meanings.

There is another type of conscious reasoning besides mental modeling, and this type of reasoning takes place individually or as part of mental models. This is the analytic reasoning, and it may be rational or not. Analytic reasoning may take place at all thinking levels. At the first level of reasoning, the analytic thinking is algorithmic, conducted directly through the common basic algorithms if-then, repeat-until. What makes the distinction between the first level analytic reasoning and the second and third level thinking is that the subject of study is not directly algorithmic in the specific instance, but algorithms are implicitly embedded within the occurring circumstance or statement.

At the second level of thinking, intuitive thinking is used to break down or cognitively digest the encountered circumstance, down to the first level of thinking which is directly algorithmic in nature, and therefore directly processed by any intelligence. Yet in order to digest cognitively the specific circumstance down to the first level, intelligences have to employ their cognitive system, and therefore they have to open inner realities within their cognitive systems, while thinking. It is similar with the third level of reasoning, when primal intelligences open inner realities that open inner realities, until the entire circumstance is digested cognitively through analytical reasoning and mental models, down to the most basic algorithmic thinking.

All primal intelligences are capable to take apart an entire environment into informational elements by specialization, replicating everything as an entire inner world, and through it, becoming able to tend separately to all needs, through their own abilities. We have seen how all intelligences do so, together with the rest of intelligences of their cognitive system, regardless of their environment. And they do so not only by monitoring and tending to their tasks, but they do so by opening on their own new inner realities, where they construct entire replicas of this replica of the environment, in order to be able to reason through them analytically. This is how cognitive systems open newer inner realities one after another, and they do so in order to break apart or digest cognitively the environment into smaller and smaller cognitive elements, down to basic, simple cognitive conceptual elements or conceptual algorithms.

And they do so in order to be able to understand these cognitive elements, store them, and then model occurrences, outcomes, or any circumstance through them. And through this highly tedious and highly complex cognitive behavior, the mind manages to break apart or digest cognitively the relevant outside environment into the smallest cognitive elements and procedures, addressing everything separately and precisely in this manner, down to the slightest conceptual detail that you are capable to understand.

And this defines the behavior of your cognitive system, and

this defines the behavior of all separate inner cognitive systems of all your inner intelligences. This defines the behavior of all higher beings from all higher worlds, and this defines the cognitive behavior of the One itself.

7 INTELLIGENT BEHAVIOR

In the first part of this book, we have modeled your physical behavior in general and your social behavior in particular. In the second part, we have modeled your cognitive behavior, which is the behavior of your subconscious and conscious intelligences while they control your individual and social behavior. This is also your own cognitive behavior as a conscious intelligence. And in this third part of the book, we model your intelligence behavior, which is your behavior as an intelligence in the outside world and within your cognitive system. We also model here your interconnective behavior within your cognitive system, within society, and in the wider world. We model your individual intelligences, how they are formed, how they develop, how they interact, how they send needs, how they specialize, and most importantly, we model how intelligences interconnect in order to live, reason, and behave together.

Your intelligence interconnective behavior is your comprehensive behavior at the level of your individual intelligences. Your intelligence interconnective behavior modeled here determines your cognitive behavior that we have just modeled last chapter. On its turn, your cognitive behavior determines and controls your individual and social behaviors, modeled in the first chapter of this book. I have structured this entire model of the human behavior differently than your lifeline of causality, in order to fulfill your interest in learning everything necessary in order for you to be able to control your comprehensive behavior through your own means, through your own reasoning, and through your own independent decisions.

This entire model of your behavior is a mental model in itself, structured specifically to be acquired easily and directly by your own inner replica of this world, with you having the chance to reason alongside it, continuously. You now understand how your behavior has specific causes determining and controlling it, you know how to identify and manage these causes at will, you are able to identify all intelligences of your cognitive system sending you your needs, you know how your environment influences your intelligences and how they influence your behavior well enough to determine you to fulfill your needs, and through your needs, to fulfill your meaning in this world, higher and lower. You know how the human mind reasons and how intelligences send you needs, and now you are ready to learn how you as an intelligence control your own behavior within your cognitive system and in the outside world. In order to do so, you have to be able to learn everything about your intelligence, as its characteristics, identity, origin, and development.

We have not modeled reasoning yet at the level of your individual intelligences, but only at the level of your cognitive system as a whole and through its primal, specialized abilities, as the eating intelligence, the conscious intelligence, the recovery intelligence, the social intelligence, and the reproductive intelligence.

What motivates your eating behavior? Why exactly do you eat? Because you feel hungry, certainly. Or this is the case under normal circumstances, because you may eat for any reason besides hunger, as for social reasons, or for gaining immediate pleasure, or because you feel bored and therefore you substitute your need for learning with your need for food, while intending to be rewarded similarly with pleasure. Why do you feel hunger? Your hunger is sent to you by your primal eating intelligence. Your eating intelligence lives its life within its own specialized library of knowledge, which is its own inner replica of this world, just as you live your life as your inner self within your own inner replica of the outside world. And this is the case because you perceive only what you know and understand in this world, while ignoring the rest. And you ignore the rest because you cannot know what you do not know, otherwise you knew it. This is how you have large gaps in your inner replica of this world without knowing it. Yet this is the case with everybody and with all intelligences, since they have their own libraries of knowledge coming in form of inner replicas of their own environment within their cognitive systems, and therefore they make mistakes.

How does your eating intelligence determine you to eat? It sends you your casual hunger, pain, pleasure, and fulfillment, feelings capable to control your entire eating behavior throughout life. In fact, these feelings match so precisely your eating behavior, that you may live an entire life subconsciously, through your feelings, without having to reason at all, while you are still successful in life, integrating perfectly in your family life and in society. Yet you still have the chance to live your life too weak or too heavy in this manner, and therefore it is recommended that you invest your reasoning in order to identify your feelings, parallel them with your reasoning and accurate knowledge but not with beliefs, and in this manner, you increase the efficiency and compatibility of your behavior.

But how exactly does your eating intelligence send you your hunger and how does it know exactly when to send it? Your eating intelligence is conscious, and within its own specialized world, it lives a very normal life, comparable to yours. Similar to you, your eating intelligence has to fulfill needs its entire life for one main purpose, to be able to manage the entire digestive system, while it feeds all cells of your body, and while it plans for future famines and excessive bodily demands, and while maintaining sufficient reserves of fat, nutrients, and water.

Compared to this extraordinarily detailed task, you as a conscious intelligence are only a simple extension of your eating intelligence, you are its ability to interact with the outside world in order to gather, cook, and eat the food that it needs. And according to its own specialized replica of this world, your eating intelligence might feel that it is the one taking the food itself from the outside world, through you the conscious intelligence.

It is relevant to state here who controls whom within your cognitive system. You may be able to control the behavior of your physical body in the outside world, yet you might not be able to control all intelligences of your cognitive system. There is a clear hierarchy of intelligences formed and active in any cognitive system, and you have to be able to identify yours throughout life, since it changes continuously, depending on various circumstances. While you have to be able to identify these circumstances. This cognitive hierarchy is never stable, and it always depends on your modes of life.

What are your modes of life? You do not behave similarly continuously throughout life, but you are capable to change settings and functions of your mind and body, in order to behave according to all changes in your environment, in a most precise and efficient manner. If it is a pleasant environment, safe and abundant, as it is the case when you come home from work, then you change settings from the rush of the traffic, and you take the chance to recover your organism through this new mode of life called the recovery mode of life. You eat and enjoy a nice family evening, and you do so through a different mode of your behavior, the recovery mode. Because your recovery intelligence stands on top of your cognitive hierarchy of intelligences right now, with your eating intelligence positioned right below it, and with your reproductive intelligence to follow, depending on your family environment.

But does the house catch on fire? Your ability to switch instantly from recovery to crisis accelerated modes of life will save yourself and your family from the disaster, because your recovery and eating intelligences are not in control of your cognitive system anymore, but you are, the conscious intelligence. While all primal intelligences of your system stay put to help you in every manner, even by stopping all their activities entirely in order to divert all energy, reasoning, and power, to your disposal. It is this type of cognitive cooperation that I encourage you to identify and maintain throughout the multitude of modes of your behavior, which you undergo in order to match the multitude of types of your environment. You may also notice this hierarchy of intelligences within your cognitive system by studying and monitoring your axis of hormones.

What is an axis of hormones? You may identify the activity of your primal intelligences through your needs, feelings, and behaviors that you undergo according to their commands. You may also trace the activity of your primal intelligences and of their current hierarchy of intelligences by identifying what hormones and neurotransmitters are present throughout your body. Hormones and neurotransmitters are arrays of proteins, amino acids, ions, and steroids holding your various primal intelligences. Sex hormones hold your reproductive intelligence through arrays of steroids, while it spreads out through blood vessels to cover your entire body, or while it exits through skin to spread outside your body as pheromones. You will notice that there are not only sex hormones present in your body, but also digestive hormones, metabolic hormones, and recovery hormones. When their hormones are present in various amounts, primal intelligences end up taking over each other's tasks according to the current mode of life, to do the job of other primal intelligences. Your primary eating intelligence usually manages the storage of fat throughout your body, yet when your body switches to the reproductive mode of life, then your reproductive intelligence climbs to the top of your hierarchy of intelligences and takes control of the entire cognitive system, and through it, of the entire organism.

Why does the reproductive intelligence take control? Sometimes the outside environment changes in its favor and it switches your current mode of life to the adult mode of life. Or sometimes, you manage to change your mode of life, always unknowingly. Probably there is a large amount of adult activity lately in your life, therefore you are about to get pregnant or this is what your primal intelligences assume, and now your body has to be reshaped and filled with fat deposits to last you throughout pregnancy, and this is what they do. All happening against your will, because you the conscious intelligence are now toward the bottom of the hierarchy of intelligences of your cognitive system, when it comes to fat deposits. It is the same with the social hierarchy of power in society. Or it was supposed to be the same, with society being led by its most capable individuals according to its own modes of society, while society is led continuously by its most selfish and incapable people.

And since everything related to reproduction, pregnancy, and raising babies is under the responsibility and control of your reproductive intelligence, now your reproductive intelligence interconnects hierarchically with your eating intelligence, subduing it, and it becomes now the one deciding the storage of fat throughout your body. Throughout different modes of life, when you are badly sick or badly harassed, your recovery or security primal intelligences will also take control of the hierarchy of intelligences of your cognitive system, in a similar manner, to rule as they need, while managing the entire organism throughout crisis, many times depositing new fat, or only relocating your current fat throughout your body.

And this is how you may also tell what is going on in your cognitive system, by the shape of your body, being as an apple or as a pear. Since it never matters what diet you go through, because you will still gain fat, for as long as you remain in these adult, sufferance, or crisis modes of life.

What can you do? Are you still in school and it is too soon to have babies? Then you have to give up your adult behavior, because you mislead all intelligences of your cognitive system. Now you have decided to go through a hard diet, you stopped cooperating, you broke the harmony within your cognitive system, you compromised your health and behavior, and you are at risk. Everything can happen to you now, because you are far from achieving your normal activity, your optimum behavior, which is your favorable mode of life, matching a third intelligent human environment.

Because you are a living human being by nature, and this is what your intelligences always expect, counting in zillions. Otherwise, in any other environment, and throughout any other mode of life and mode of behavior, you destabilize your intelligences, you break the harmony, they punish you, you feel dreadfully, you take drugs to compensate instead of seeking to regain your third level human homeostasis and modes of life, and so you suffer some more, even indefinitely. Because you never learn in school of all these, but they only teach you about consensual servitude and animal behavior. They even teach you that you are an animal, and a servant. While they even give you drugs, compromising everything.

How does the eating intelligence know what food to ask for through the needs that it sends you? How does it know when to send them? It does so according to its own specialized inner replica of this world. And as we have seen, its inner world is very vast, since it has the precision and resolution of subcellular details and even of molecular details. But how does the eating intelligence know what to do and when? Its specialized world changes according to anything that cells need in what it concerns materials and energy, being needed in form of nutrients and calories. But how?

What happens is that the outside and the inside of your organism are not exactly as biology teaches, or as doctors see them when they perform surgery. As we have seen throughout all models if this book series, there is a correspondent duality always present in all living beings, since they are both physically objective, and cognitively intelligent. Therefore, living beings experience two types of existence simultaneously, objective and subjective, or real and cognitive, and they are always capable to exist in any one, or in both simultaneously. Your eating intelligence manages everything related to food throughout your body, and you can see it at work in a physical manner through the multitude of its glands, organs, hormones, neurotransmitters, movement of food, fat deposits, and gastric juices. While there is an even more intense cognitive activity going on throughout the body and throughout cells, paralleling this physical activity everywhere. And while all the physical activity of your eating intelligence is continuously interconnected and predictable everywhere, it is the same with its cognitive activity, it is interconnected in a very similar manner, also interconnecting with all cellular activity, which includes cellular food management. While both the real and the cognitive worlds look very similar since they are correspondent, while they superimpose most of the time. Because in their own cognitive world, intelligences can see and interact with needs and feelings in a tangible, objective manner, while thoughts are simple changes in their own physical environment.

How does the eating intelligence send you your hunger from a cognitive perspective? It simply takes the food that it needs from its own real, objective world, it takes the food from wherever it is located in its cognitive fridge and shelves of your grocery store, it takes it from there as it pleases, and consequently, now you feel this incredible feeling to go to your fridge and make a sandwich, not knowing that you copycat your own eating intelligence in your real world.

And there is more taking place, because your primal intelligences lack your advanced reasoning capabilities. They are not capable to perceive and understand the outside world as you do, but they understand it through you, through your own reasoning and replica of this world. And this marks the difference between what you expect and what you have within your cognitive system. And you always have to account for this. And this is why your primal intelligences cannot distinguish between facts and fiction or between the real and the imaginary, and you must always tell them what is real and what is imaginary. If not, then your primal intelligences consider everything to be real, they switch you from one mode of life to another unnecessarily while matching your stories, books, daydreams, and movies, and life may become too chaotic in this manner, out of control. If you watch a horror movie and you feel hunger, it is because your body is preparing to go through the entire excessive trauma from the movie. If you only tell your subconscious mind that it is not real, you may be surprised to feel how your hunger goes away. But then your security intelligence stops sending you dopamine and adrenaline, and without these, you do not feel entertained anymore, as the movie makes no sense, because it is garbage anyway. It was for the adrenaline and the dopamine that you were watching the movie, in order to feel good. Is this selfishness? Because your primal intelligences were probably waiting for mandatory tasks that you were supposed to take care of since last Tuesday.

And this is exactly how life gets out of control, through this lack of harmony, cooperation, and concordance within your cognitive system, because you tend to live your life in order to feel good, while your primal intelligences make use of your addiction to pleasure in order to subdue and control you throughout their cognitive hierarchy of intelligences only for you to be disposed to fulfill their needs. Because if you do not, you die. Even more, since you are a highly capable reasoning living being, you can always find ways to bypass your primal intelligences in order to receive your pleasure directly as you wish, through drugs and entertainment. And society provides these greatly, in order to keep you diverted, disconnected, and underdeveloped. Or you may subdue your primal intelligences to force them to give you pleasure themselves. Or you may trick your primal intelligences in every manner in order to give you pleasure, by tempering with what they consider to be real in this world, and so you receive your pleasure.

And here is the key to understand everything, because you never seek to feel good throughout life despite of what you learn from music and TV, but you always seek to feel better. Because this is how pleasure works, otherwise you get bored through a constant amount of pleasure, since it feels the same. And this is why pleasure is addictive, by default. And it is meant to be in this manner, in order for you to be always very motivated to fulfill your needs. Or this is the case at the second developmental level, which is the animal level. Because you want to feel better and better, you want more and more pleasure, and you ruin your mind and body in the process, in every manner.

Or at least, this is the case with the endorphins that give you pleasure, because serotonins and oxytocin are different. Because these two are used as rewards for different circumstances, as long-term rewards. While dopamine is more of a stimulant and a rusher than a reward, and therefore it is just as harmful as endorphins. You have to be able to identify where your pleasure comes from, through what neurotransmitters, and for what reasons, otherwise, you may end up harming yourself while losing control of your life and behavior, only because you try to feel better for five minutes longer.

Would you like to know more about your escalating need for pleasure? Do this now. Take a few moments now to scan your pleasure throughout your mind, and throughout your body. You will find tension everywhere pleasure is present, since you divert in this manner blood and resources to fuel your pleasure abundantly, in order for you to receive more intense pleasure, unknowingly. Try to cancel your pleasure now at once, everywhere, or gradually, wherever you find it, while relaxing all tensed places of the mind and body. Let the blood flow freely, and allow your body to enter a complete recovery mode of life. Breathe deeply, just as necessarily, while trying to feel normal and neutral, without tension, pleasure, or pain. Only neutral and relaxed, without feelings, without any problems. Let your eyes relax, even as you continue reading. Always breathe deeply and sufficiently. Eliminate all tension, all pleasure, and all feelings, but keep only love and happiness. Do not temper with the level of your love and happiness, just let them be. Relax your face and throat, breathe deeply, and relax. Do not worry, since absence of pleasure will not ruin your life, as you keep your love and happiness at normal levels. Relax your eyes deeply. You may take a few minutes now to relax, or you may go to the next paragraph.

You may notice the low, tensed pleasure going away. This is endorphin, it is actually a stress hormone, it is always addictive, and many times, you have to pay it back with depression, pain, phobia, and hangover when it is over. This happens because you have fulfilled the wrong need, and you are punished for not fulfilling the actual need instead. This happens when you drink alcohol, because alcohol has its own endorphins in it. It also happens when you eat unnecessarily or excessively, because you receive endorphins from your intestines when you eat, along with serotonin, if you eat adequately. You also pay back with boredom and distress your endorphins after you are entertained in any manner, while you were supposed to fulfill your higher level human needs. Relax this low pleasure now, and let it go away. You are in your recovery mode of life now, and in your third level intelligent human developmental mode of life, simultaneously.

If you have just found out that you have been tensing your face, eyes, throat, brain, and shoulders strongly for years now, in order to receive your pleasure continuously, this is very common. Wrinkles show up in this manner, along with pain all over the body, along with skeletal deformation, atherosclerosis, and myopia. The high pleasure that you feel instead is actually happiness, it is lower in intensity, but it feels higher and fulfilling. You might want to keep it, yet it is a long-term good feeling, and it comes back anyway, along with love. Love is a longer-term reward for social interconnectivity and for reproduction, in order to remain around your loved ones, for various reasons.

By now, you should notice how you cannot remove your pleasure from your body, since it comes back. These are happiness and love coming back most of the time, along with pleasure, and you should be able to distinguish them individually. Besides, they come through different hormones and neurotransmitters, as endorphins for pleasure, serotonins for happiness, and oxytocin for love. You may want to allow your primal intelligences to have a rest, to recover themselves, to replenish with energy, and you may do so by remaining ahead of their needs, as through eating properly, regularly, in sufficient amounts, only as main meals, three times a day, nutritionally diverse, just as you feel, and eating nothing between meals. You may also slow down or stop these hormones and feelings, including the good ones, to allow your primal intelligences to rest, recover, and to tend to their own tasks.

And this is the difference between animals and humans, between second level beings and third level intelligent human beings, because once the second level beings are guided by needs and feelings continuously throughout life, humans reason and feel, because humans are thinkers more than feelers, humans are intelligent more than sentient, because humans can manage their feelings along with their needs, tasks, and meanings, through advanced, continuous reasoning.

Try it now, to see how you cannot remove your good feelings entirely, since they always return, many times amplified. If you happen to feel now a slight, constant high feeling of bliss or happiness everywhere within you and all around, or slightly above your head, that is exactly how it feels to be human, or that may be your soul, or Life herself, depending how high you are capable to reach through your conscious, subconscious, and highconscious selves.

You do not have to take drugs as caffeine, alcohol, or stronger, to feel good, since you receive your good feelings anyway, by managing them, by controlling them, by remaining ahead of your needs and tasks, and by maintaining harmony within your cognitive system. Yet you have to know everything about your body and mind in order to stay ahead, which may not be possible. And this is how you have to rely on your primal intelligences, because together, you know everything. And since they are alive and intelligent, you have to treat your primal intelligences as people and not as mechanisms, not as slaves, not as animals, and not even as adults. Your primal intelligences are more as children, they get upset easily yet they forgive you, they love you and they care for you, and you should do the same, since you live your life together. In fact, your primal intelligences together are exactly the child you were before, just because your conscious intelligence was not developed then, and you were living your life through your primal intelligences. You were playing through them, and many times, you were playing with them, while they were making everything seem real. And it was fun, while you were teaching them about the real world, and while they were teaching you about life, needs, and reasoning. This is the kind of cognitive harmony that you have to maintain throughout life and not only during childhood. Now you may use your reasoning, so you do not have to play. Because back then, you could enter their cognitive world through playing, while now you can maintain the harmony both in the real world and in the cognitive world.

Try now to see if you can return to your third level studying and reasoning modes of life, since you are already in your playing and recovery modes of life, from the above paragraphs. If you do not return to your third level human learning mode of life, you cannot understand the book as you did so far. You do not have to tense your body, but you just have to switch back to learning, by privileging your mind and reasoning, while still keeping your mind and body relaxed, your pleasure low, and your breathing adequately. With your eyes always relaxed and recovering.

Notice how with each one of your modes of life, your behavior changes accordingly, since these are also your modes of behavior. And now you might want to learn how to switch to your higher modes of life and modes of behavior, as your creative mode of life.

To get back to watching movies for pleasure, the problem is not that you have to eat sandwich with chips at night while doing so unnecessarily, but your eating intelligence switches you entirely to a food overstocking mode of life, because of the cataclysm from the movie and the famine soon to follow, and now you must eat all the food that you can find, and to store it in your body as fat. What can you do? Just find ways to remain within third level human modes of life, since in this manner you skip the second level animal modes of life, along with all extreme modes of life, including the fat overstocking mode of life. You do so by keeping your real and consensual environments neutral and at the third, human level, by assuring your subconscious that the movie was not real, by earning your trust within your cognitive system, and now by waiting patiently for your eating intelligence to get down from the top of your cognitive hierarchy of intelligences, and therefore to switch you back to your third level human modes of life.

Why do you always have to take care that your environment is of the third, human level? Because only then, you are certain that you remain at the top of the cognitive hierarchy of intelligences, while studying relevant knowledge, performing art, writing books, making documentaries or movies, helping others, cooperating with others toward making a better world, seeking righteousness in this world, and remaining independent.

Can you really talk with your subconscious mind? Yes, since your intelligences can hear and understand your words, and can follow your thoughts. They can even answer you through needs, feelings, and ideas popping up in your mind, or even in more intelligent manners, if you are more developed. But if your intelligences are very developed, and they speak in words, do not tell anyone, since you end up medicated, and they never speak to you again, since they lose this ability. But can this be possible? All intelligences understand words, as they can even read them. Just study closely the word 'lemon' right now to see it for yourself.

You notice how your primal eating intelligence reads it first and reacts before you even have the chance to read it yourself as a conscious intelligence. But if we study closely the word 'snake,' we notice how the security primal intelligence becomes involved immediately. But if we study closely the words 'monster from the horror movie,' all your intelligences are ready for the entire entertainment of the horror movie, bringing in the popcorn. Regardless of the fact that the monsters from horror movies should be significantly more terrifying than the little snakes from the real world.

You have to be an intelligent human being first, at your third developmental level, before you even start aspiring to develop to your fourth developmental level. Because if you are not an intelligent human being, if you are still taking drugs at the zero level, if you are still taking orders from others at the first level, or if you are still engaged in a tight social competition at your second level, then once you unleash the powers of your higher mind, you lose control, you create demons instead of goodness in this world, you end up enslaving this world instead of freeing it, and this world will never forgive you. And this world will try to eliminate you. Just take it gradually, first solve your sickness, drugs, and medication, then solve your servitude problems, then solve your subconscious, uncontrollable instincts and behavior, then ascend to the intelligent human level and live your life through an intelligent human behavior, then bring the entire society to the intelligent human society level, and then aspire to your fourth developmental level, to manage your highconscious world. And it can be done.

How do primal intelligences behave, interact, interconnect, and communicate? The eating intelligence knows through its immediate habitat of its cognitive world what it needs and in what quantity, and through its own mental models that it conducts in its cognitive habitat, it can predict what it is going to need hours and even days in advance. This is how you know what to buy for the week when you go grocery shopping, because your eating intelligence will tell you. If you monitor your communication with your eating intelligence that you have when you go grocery shopping, you will be surprised of how complex it is, how you two bargain and make compromises, how you two love and hate each other while you do so, and it might even seem funny, but you do not actually feel alone anymore. Because you manage to interconnect intrinsically with all your primal intelligences and it feels unique, since it is just as in our example with Rebecca. Because your zillion specialized intelligences working around the clock while tending to all tasks of the organism, family, and society are more than what they do, but they are priceless, unique, and even fragile living beings.

How priceless and how unique are your intelligences? You cannot tell it on your own intelligences, since you always had them with you, and you are used with them by now. But you can tell it in your loved ones, since by now, you know well all their primal subconscious intelligences, just as much as you know them the conscious intelligences.

Yet there is a way to tell. Because whenever you harm drastically the specific area of the left prefrontal cortex where the intelligent inner self lives, you end up with total amnesia, since you actually die, because that was you. But then, the new intelligence from the surrounding cortex area replacing you and taking over your intelligent specialization of interacting with the outside world while fulfilling needs has entirely different personality traits and cognitive characteristics, making you be an entirely different living human being.

Because these are our intelligences, and they are actually us, in all our details, characteristics, and entire personalities. And right now, as you scan your cognitive system, you may certainly identify all your intelligences, exactly as they are, the actual unique living beings that they actually are. While they are not exactly at the age of the physical body, but they are actually eternal, staying alive and successful since the dawn of life. And this is why they are flawless with each need and meaning that they send you, because they have been doing so since the dawn of life, and they know well what they do.

How does your eating intelligence know how much food it needs when it sends you your needs? How does it know of what nutritious type it must be, mostly when this food that you eat is meant to match your future activity for the next twenty-four hours or more? How can it predict the type and intensity of your behavior in order to match it with the precise energy and nutrients that it is going to require from you to cook and eat? Your eating intelligence has direct access to your senses of perception, and it can perceive the outside environment, helping it to decide. Your eating intelligence can also listen to you conversations in the family and in society, it can see you thinking and deciding within the inner cognitive world, it can see your mental models and your ideas, plans, and decisions there, and it will even wait patiently until you have well decided your important future activity, before it asks you through an increased appetite to eat more. And this is exactly how you adapt to your future environment, since you plan for it through your mental models. Only that your primal intelligences might even live their lives directly in the future, throughout their specialized inner replicas of this world, just to be able to remain ahead of all problems, and just to be able to remain in control of all future events, regardless of how unpredictable they may become. And since realities have different continuums and time never corresponds from one to another, who knows, primal intelligences might manage to live their lives entirely in the future, in the future of this world.

And this is how you are capable to cope with your environment precisely, by simply matching it with your behavior, by simply integrating in it naturally, by cooperating and by maintaining the harmony. And once you are capable to maintain your inner harmony with your own intelligences, just watch your loved ones gathering around you, since you are capable to maintain your outer harmony with them just as well, and with the entire world.

Do you always keep the harmony? The problems that your eating intelligence has with you, and it is similar with all your primal intelligences, is that you tend to skip the important food items that you should eat, and that the food that it demands from you to eat is altered with poisonous additives or it lacks exactly the nutrients that it needs. Because the actual food is empty, having only the color and flavor but not the content, and it has to eat again. Another problem is that you tend to waste unnecessary energy and nutrients in places as the gym, you tend to eat very little, you eat artificial food along with food additives that drug it and darken its cognitive world so much, that it cannot make sense anymore of what is in there. And all food is in this manner. And you never listen, no matter how many needs it sends you, no matter how intense they are, no matter how much it punishes you, because you still do not eat. And it hurts, it hurts them, because you never listen. And it is very frustrating.

Or this is the case with the eating intelligences living in the West, because in many eastern nations, they enjoy the inner harmony of the cognitive system more often, and it is beautiful. Unless they live in dictatorships, spooked up the entire time, with the stomach so tensed, that they can barely use the bathroom. While in the poor nations, eating intelligences stay busy continuously, since famines and crises will return this year, killing again.

And now you can tell how intelligences are more alive than the physical bodies holding them. Even more, as you already notice, the entire behavior studied in this book, is not exactly coming from the physical bodies, and not even from the living beings themselves, but from intelligences directly, many times matching their own behavior throughout the cognitive system.

While if you have always assumed that your entire behavior in the outside world is conscious, coming from you the conscious intelligence, think again, because some or most of your behavior is directly subconscious, coming from the multitude of your subconscious intelligences. While it is worse when your body is switched to extreme modes of life, as your extreme eating modes of life, extreme fear, or extreme reproduction, since you cannot control your own behavior consciously anymore.

Therefore, according to what your future activities demand, your eating intelligence requires more or less food from you to eat, food of a specific types of nutrients. It is interesting to monitor your eating intelligence, how it sends you your hunger and for what reasons, because it is always easy to tell. Yet this is its predicting behavior, because it usually follows what your cells need at that specific time or shortly ahead of time, or it follows its own routines, or it matches everybody else, since people tend to eat together, at very precise times, and in sufficient amounts.

How does the eating intelligence see the cells and knows what they need? They interact directly, together, in their inner, cognitive world. Because for them, their cognitive world is just as real and just as objective as this world is out here.

But there is more to consider, since the comprehensive primal subconscious eating intelligence is actually a comprehensive cellular intelligence, made in a living, intelligent manner by the zillions of eating cellular intelligences, now spanning the entire organism and tending to all cells of the organism. While all these cellular and subcellular eating intelligences know very well what they need, with the precision of molecules, for all cells and cellular components of the entire organism, counting in zillions. It is an extraordinary complexity, yet it is not as impossible to take place as it seems, since life folds upon itself through entire forms of life and classes of life to make everything possible.

Because you always have the organic form of life sitting on top of the cellular form of life, with all overall primal intelligences spanning the entire organism composed minutely by all relevant cellular intelligences from the cellular form of life. But then, you have the cellular form of life sitting on top of the molecular form of life, having again the overall cellular intelligences formed minutely by all inner intelligences of all molecules of the molecular form of life, since molecular intelligences are formed by the inner intelligences of all ions and amino acids, with them standing on top of even lower forms of life, down to the raw field or Universal Mind, where all intelligences of the wider world have their roots or origin.

The cells of your body interconnect in a specific manner to create the primal eating intelligence, along with the rest of the cognitive system, just as the neurons of your brain interconnect physically in order to make possible your existence and cognitive activity as a conscious intelligence. What happens is that cellular membranes are not exactly solid walls, since nothing is material and solid at that very small scale, but it is only field and intelligences. Cellular membranes are plasmatic or ionic in nature, and they are capable to hold intelligences by vibrating in the field and therefore by interacting with the field. Free ions found between cells are capable to unite cellular membranes in order to help them interconnect in a genuine array spanning the entire tissue, the entire organ, the entire system, and even the entire organism, depending on circumstances, many times interconnecting with the brain, depending on circumstances. These overall ionic membranes hold the primal intelligences, while you may also consider that the primal intelligences themselves are the specific bodily systems, as the digestive system.

Because everything is intelligence in your organism. Because everything is alive in your body, being both intelligence and physical or organic. Because your organism is not divided into your brain and the rest of the body despite of what science may claim, but your organism is your cognitive system entirely, and nothing else. Because you the conscious intelligence are but a few neurons found in the left prefrontal cortex if you happen to be right-handed, while the rest is your subconscious mind. And since your subconscious mind is made of your other primal intelligences entirely, and since these are the individual systems of your body that spread everywhere in the body, it is not possible to differentiate between the brain and the rest of the body anymore.

The brain is part of the nervous system, yet the nervous system is used by all primal intelligences as it covers the entire organism. The difference between neurons and regular, specialized cells is that neurons are capable to elongate or morph their physical shape into axons and dendrites in order to be able to reach and interconnect ionically through axons and dendrites with other neurons or regular cells, while regular cells have to interconnect ionically through all cells caught in between while forming the overall ionic membrane, using these as relays, while making them do the relay work unnecessarily. You can even see on an EEG display the overall ironic cellular membrane instating itself shortly throughout the organism, as it does so for animals and plants alike.

These interconnected cells become the body of your eating intelligence not permanently, but only as needed, while the eating intelligence is the overall intelligence in itself. And when you have body and intelligence, you have life. The eating intelligence is alive, just as alive as you are, the conscious intelligence. While it is significantly vaster than you are, and therefore more capable.

The eating intelligence receives its needs directly from all the cells of the body, trillions of them. Your cells send feelings throughout your body to all intelligences assembling to form the specific cognitive hierarchy of intelligences that involves the current feeding endeavor, and this hierarchy certainly includes the eating and conscious intelligences. You are in this together in what it concerns your feelings, all your intelligences, and you send and receive feelings throughout the cognitive system whenever you have to. And when you do, you send feelings to all intelligences of your cognitive system and they feel them, and they respond according to their hierarchical position, always knowing what happens everywhere. And this makes for a highly coordinated cognitive behavior throughout life, leading to the casual physical behavior that you normally undergo. Do your part in all cognitive systems of intelligences, and you maintain the harmony.

You find cognitive hierarchies of intelligences throughout all second level cognitive systems. Third level cognitive systems may include advanced reasoning, meant to bypass the continuous, direct enforcement of orders done through feelings. At the same time, feelings are good and bad, rewarding or punishing. When you use your reasoning, and therefore when you are capable to maintain your cognitive system in the rewarding state of your punishment-reward mechanism, then you are on your way toward a third level cognitive system. In order to do so, you have to reason and remain ahead of your needs, tasks, and requirements throughout life, which is a genuine third level human behavior.

Which in turn assures a third level cognitive system. Everything is interconnected, everything has to be at the third level, and in general, continuous love and happiness in life means high developmental achievement.

Yet you can never seek only love and happiness throughout life in order to ascend to your third level behavior, since love and happiness are only effects, they are your rewards for your highly developed behavior. You have to be highly developed in order to be able to undergo a genuine third level human behavior, and then in order to be rewarded continuously with love and happiness. And this is the mistake that people make in society, because they seek love and happiness along with the rest of the good feelings while they ignore their continuous need for development, which is the main cause and the main requirement for all these to happen.

'Love is all you need.' Yet this is not entirely true, since love is an effect, a simple reward, while you have to address the main causes from your lifeline of causality, as having a loving, proper human environment, along with cognitive harmony and cooperation within your cognitive system, along with an entire cognitive system already developed at the third level, along with intelligent human reasoning, along with intelligent human knowledge and an intelligent human development taking place continuously, all resulting in a genuine third level human behavior. And it is through this highly developed behavior that you are capable to fulfill your needs, and only then, you receive your continuous love and happiness as a reward.

Love is all you need. Yet as we see, if you fail to consider everything preceding love itself, then your life goes terribly out of control. Because it is not an easy task to be and remain human, since the entire consensual human society is in competition against you. Love is all you need. Because you need more to consider throughout life. If you expect only love from life without being able to create it and maintain it yourself, you will end up addicted, with hate all around, and with your life and behavior entirely out of control. And this is exactly how people end up. Is it a coincidence that that song appeared at the same time with all drugs? And if you study history and society closely, you find how that was the time when all problems started, when everything went south.

How do cells send needs? Cells broadcast needs in form of messenger proteins called hormones and neurotransmitters, or they may broadcast their needs in form of ions, amino acids, or entire steroids, all produced in cells or in glands. These needs are more as nagging. When one cell is in need of something, it is only a local problem and the cell must manage it on its own or it dies and it is recycled. But when an entire tissue of cells, or the entire organ, or the entire organism of cells nag for food, then the eating intelligence must respond, and it has to find food in the outside world through you the conscious intelligence, it has to eat it, digest it, and then send it to the tissue or organ in demand, or to the entire organism. Or if food is not available, it takes fat, minerals, and vitamins from the storage, and then it uses these to produce calories along with most of the needed nutrients.

How do cells know how to send needs? Are cells intelligent? Does this mean that cells are alive? biology claims that only organisms are alive. And if cells are intelligent, then how exactly do they think? Only neurons are capable to think, according to science, and they are not considered by science alive, since they are not organisms. Spirituality claims that everything is alive, including cells and organs, along with mountains and seas, yet these are beliefs and we cannot integrate them in our model. And then, how do cells interconnect to form intelligences, in order to send and receive needs?

To consider your recovery intelligence now, your cells send their needs for recovery, maintenance, and division throughout the body, while your recovery intelligence has to tend to them. Your recovery intelligence is also a primal subconscious intelligence, as your eating intelligence. The difference between regular intelligences and primal intelligences is that primal intelligences do not die. Or they have never died, while they have always been the prime abilities of the subconscious mind.

Your primal recovery subconscious intelligence contains your immune system, your recovery system, and your cellular division system, all in one. Your cells again send their messenger proteins whenever they are tired and had enough and it is time to take a break in order to tend to themselves, while you feel it as fatigue, weakness, sleep, loss in energy, and lower metabolism.

You also become tired throughout your intense physical or cognitive behavior and need to rest and wait to regain your breath, yet cells are different than organisms. Cells also have to work throughout life, they tend to their specialization, but they cannot do so continuously as you may assume. Cells are composed of billions of cellular components that may have lifespans measuring in hours or minutes. These need continuous maintenance and replacement. Cells need nutrients in order to recover, as you have to eat these if you can find them, since most of them are essential nutrients, and they are hard to find, as the omega acids needed for the maintenance of cellular membranes and steroids, and it takes time to recover. While many times, cells cannot work and recover themselves simultaneously, or at least not at the optimum performance that you may expect. And when you take dopamine or caffeine, you force your cells to go through supercharged modes of life unnecessarily, for your pure pleasure. They suffer damages and exhaust in this manner, and they have to recover soon, while soon is exactly the time when you want them to be sharp again and to work hard in order to match your new intense behavior, or because you had another coffee and drinks with your other friends. Many cells cannot do so, and they die and are recycled. While you feel pain in the stomach, heart, and muscles in general, so you take even more drugs, prescribed. And this is the zero developmental level, mostly when you have zero knowledge about all these.

A problem is that all primal intelligences take time from your recovery in order to fulfill their needs. While your reproductive primal intelligence always does so. Because there are dreadful implications when cells are not allowed to tend to themselves on time and for as long as they need, or they die. And then you have to make new cells, and it is even more time consuming, while you become weak and sick, and you lose nutrients. And it is not the fault of the recovery primal intelligence either, yet this happens only because the recovery primal intelligence can always postpone its activity on behalf of the rest of the primal intelligences, and so it always does.

If you study this case, you find the problem to be in society, because society does not allow enough time for you to tend to your other needs. And when society states what you have to do and when, you have to do so, or else.

Do you seek to control your behavior and your life? Then you have to maintain harmony and cooperation within your cognitive system, within your body, within society, and within nature. And while your behavior integrates in your environment, then your behavior becomes harmonious and therefore manageable. How do you maintain harmony and cooperation? You have to know everything about your mind, body, society, and nature, and these are your environment. More importantly, you have to know accurate facts and not beliefs, because beliefs may tell you to do everything imaginable and you do so, it will not work, and you end up harming yourself irreparably.

What facts? In order to maintain harmony, you have to cooperate with all your primal intelligences yourself, just as they cooperate with you continuously throughout life. Do not take time and resources from them, or they become dysfunctional soon, and your health, mind, body, and behavior decay consequently. Sleep longer, avoid all drugs and chemicals, be careful not to harm yourself and others in any manner, be nice with your cells and intelligences because they are alive, exercise every morning when you wake up for fifteen minutes or so, be careful with what you eat and with what you say, maintain a positive, constructive environment and attitude all around, manage your feelings keeping your pleasure low, and more importantly, relax deeply daily, whenever you happen to lay down, mostly while you read your books.

Recovery also involves the actual recovery from sickness, which is done through the immune system. This involves prevention, protection, sickness detection, sickness and infection eradication, and recovery. The model for the human health is very complex and tedious to know and master.

And again, how exactly do your cells know what they need? How do they know how to tend to themselves, and how do they know how to unite themselves while asking for their needs to be fulfilled? And once they receive their energy and materials, how exactly do they know how to put them together in form of entire cells? Cells are simple, lifeless mechanisms, or this is what biology claims. Cells have their blueprints of RNA and DNA, so this should suffice to explain their behavior, yet it does not. Cells are very complex themselves, just as complex as the organism that they form. Cells are alive, and it is their life and intelligence that we have to model in order to understand their behavior, because now their behavior influences your own conscious behavior. Yet as we will see soon, all cellular components are alive, and they have their own intelligence. There is a continuous, comprehensive living behavior all around, within you and everywhere outside, and you cannot manage one without understanding the rest, since they are interconnected.

And about your reproductive intelligence having to take time from your sleep, it has nothing romantic to do with it, since you may undergo your romantic behavior everywhere and at all time, in private and in society, but not only at night in your bed. It is a social stereotype to have it at night, only in private, only with the same partner, and only with one partner, while you take time from your sleep.

The current consensual society does not accept anything reproductive to be moral and even legal. You have less children in this manner or none at all, your genetic line dies, while the genetic lines of those controlling society prosper, diversify, and expand rapidly to span the Earth, without you and your children. This is called genocide, and it is done by you to you, since you are the one censoring your behavior yourself in every manner. As it is this specific censorship of your behavior altering your inner harmony, because your reproductive intelligence will never leave you alone until you have those children, with the exact people that it chooses for you, regardless of social laws and norms. What can you do?

And now, how exactly does your reproductive intelligence know how, why, and when to send you your reproduction needs? Are the cells sending these needs intelligent too? How do they know when to send them? How do cellular intelligences know what is good and what is bad for you and for your descendants several generations down the line? Is sexual intercourse even accepted in society and in life anymore? Why would your cells and intelligences demand anything from you that defines all your time and effort throughout life, getting you badly in trouble? Are they against you?

Yet it is the best thing in this world to have and raise children, and it is the same reproductive intelligence giving you the feeling of love and completion when it comes to having, raising, and educating children. Children are good for your genetic line. Yet children are your genetic line, but how does the reproductive intelligence know what is good for your genetic line and what is not good, when genetic lines span generations in the future and in the past, while the cells composing your reproductive intelligence have a life measured in days? While reproductive intelligences are strongly determined to engage you in reproductive activities with everybody and everywhere, sending you the best rewards ever when you do, so intense, that they fry up your brains. And then when it comes to reproduction, all primal intelligences interconnect in one, providing everything necessary in order for you to attract mates, to interact with them, to prepare for pregnancy, to give birth, and then to raise and educate children, as though reproduction is your greatest meaning in life. Which is your greatest meaning, but not according to society, since society is always glad to kill your unborn children at the clinic, by the dozens throughout life. How do cells know what is good for your entire genetic line and for the entire humankind?

What we may remark now is that life is not exactly lived at your own level, which is the level of the organism, but it is lived at the level of your cells. Yet life is lived at the level of all classes of life simultaneously, and there are countless of these besides the organism class, social class, and cellular class. And by the way these interconnect in order to fulfill meanings that apply to other levels of life and not to them, while sacrificing themselves in the process sometimes in order to fulfill what it seems to be common behavior at the level of other classes of life, it seems that life is lived mostly at the level of your cells, while the entire organism only fulfills their needs.

Yet we will see soon how cells form organisms only to be able to fulfill their needs through the organism and as an organism, with more certainty. This is also why people live life in society, because they are able to fulfill their needs better, easier, and with more certainty. Yet what you always assumed and expected was that cells are just there to compose your body and to provide all the necessary inner work that you need in life, while you can always do everything you please with your body since it is your body. As you will see, even cellular components are alive, and therefore there are now zillions of living beings within you, which do not really work on your behalf, but that you have to tend to entirely, throughout life. And now, with them being alive, unique, and therefore unpredictable, by the zillions, your comprehensive behavior becomes just as unpredictable as theirs.

As a remark, intelligences and individual living beings do not unite entirely into higher classes of life while forming them, but intelligences and individuals in general still maintain their individuality within higher classes of life, and this is the case with both the human organism and the human society. Cells keep their intelligences and individuality within organisms. You are an example here, since you live within your left prefrontal cortex as you are a neural intelligence there, while for the entire organism, you are the entire conscious intelligence. While for the outside world, you are the entire organism.

Individuals within societies do not unite themselves entirely, but they keep their individuality. And even when they end up leading the entire society, they do so as individuals, as part of society themselves. While when they control the entire society, they do so through their conscious intelligence if they are more developed cognitively, or they control society through their subconscious primal intelligences, as they do when they follow their personal interests more than the interests of the entire society. And everybody does so, since they live their lives on lower developmental levels, through primal intelligences. And this is how now one neuron distinguishes itself well enough among the rest to become the leader of an entire primal intelligence, primal intelligence distinguishing itself well enough to control an entire organism throughout an entire mode of life. And when this happens to be the organism of a ruler or tyrant in society, then this little neuron with its unique, highly capable intelligence, achieves to control and determine the lives and behaviors of billions of people, also deciding who lives and who dies.

Because it seems that life is lived by individual intelligences on behalf of all classes of life above, and not the other way around. This is another type of interconnective behavior, and it transcends classes of life and realities vertically. While all members of classes of life as organisms and societies interconnect with each other in a horizontal manner. And as we have seen, this horizontal interconnection is not total as you may expect cells to interconnect within bodies, but it is only partial, and many times, it is indirect or implicit, as it is the case with people in society.

We have to study individual intelligences along with their entire behavior, if we can only find them. I refer to these as intelligences, yet at their own subjective existential level, they are genuine living beings, having a real body, an identity, a life, an environment, a behavior, and more importantly, having a well-defined meaning. Yet intelligences also think, and therefore they have a cognitive system, formed of smaller inner intelligences. Where are the smallest, individual intelligences? How far do we have to go down the existential line of inner realities in order to find individual intelligences? Let us see.

194

8 YOUR DEVELOPMENTAL BEHAVIOR AND YOUR MEANING IN LIFE

We want to study and understand the behavior of individual intelligences now, while we cannot find individual intelligences to study, but only cognitive systems full of intelligences or systems of intelligences. How can we manage to perceive, study, model, and understand cognitive activities in minute cognitive details without finding individual intelligences to study? We can create intelligences from scratch, out of the empty field, and then we have to follow them as they develop throughout time all the way to the present, in order to follow along their behavior. Which means that we have to cover life and existence continuously, along with the interconnectivity of all intelligences and of all living beings, as they develop. And now our model becomes very demanding.

Let us create an individual intelligence now, out of nothing. Or out of the field, which is the gravitational and electromagnetic field. Which is the Universal Mind here in this world. Our intelligence has to exist, and therefore at the moment of creation, it has to click simply into existence. Existence is relatively simple to understand. Objects and subjects exist or do not exist. The One is everything that exists, and therefore everything within the One exists, while everything outside the One does not exist. Therefore, when we place a rock on an empty table, the rock exists.

Existence is subjective, objective, and highjective. We want to create an objective living being in order to study its intelligence, and then we hope to be able to develop it to a human being, in order to address these studies to you and to your intelligence. Because right now, we seek to create a model for the human being, only to be able to study its intelligences individually, along with their reasoning and behavior. We may create a subjective body, in our mind or on a laptop, but we cannot develop this into a real living being, without an intelligence.

We are touching here the everlasting debate between creationism and evolution, while it is not our intention. What happened during creation is that the Divine created the entire world at once, while he did so from a higher reality. Therefore, all living beings that he created are subjective in nature from his perspective, along with this entire world. We want to create an objective living being, and we want to do so from here, from within our world. While evolution does not help, since evolution is not a model of the actual evolution of species, but it is only a remark or an assumption: species evolve. But how did everything start? Where is that first intelligence ever, so we can find it and study it now? Because it has to be an individual intelligence, which is exactly what we need to study. Religion and spirituality state that the first intelligence was divine in nature, part of the intelligence of the Divine himself, part of the One. This means that life and intelligence have always existed, and have always been part of the One. Which implies that we will never find our individual intelligence, since it will always be part of a cognitive system, part of a larger system of intelligences. Which finally implies that intelligences in themselves are always systems of intelligences, similar to civilizations. We keep this result flexible within our model, since it is based on religious and spiritual beliefs.

Our finding may seem trivial, yet it states whether

intelligences are born or created, it states how they are born or created, and it states how they die. Because as systems of intelligences, intelligences may split into parts or samples of themselves in order to create new intelligences. This happens with cells when they divide, while cells are alive. This also happens with civilizations when they colonize new places, forming in time new civilizations. And since civilizations are higher classes of life, in themselves, they are alive.

Is this true? Are civilizations alive in themselves? Are you, the organism alive yourself, as a class of life formed by living cells? You are only assuming yourself alive, yet your cells are alive, not your organism in itself. And this is the case just because you are the conscious intelligence, residing in a small group of neurons. You are a cell, and this is why you are alive. Which means that you are alive through your cells, and not through your organism, which may be considered a community of cells. However, Life considers all her classes alive, including your organism, along with society and the human civilization. And this is the case because cells in themselves are communities of living cellular components, and therefore they could not be alive either, but only unions of living beings. Study yourself again as a conscious intelligence, to find yourself not being one neuron either, but being a neural component. If you are alive, then that is alive, and nothing else. While cellular components are also formed of smaller living beings, while you can never find the smallest, individual living being either, to define it as the main living being, but only classes of life that hold systems of intelligences. Cells are composed of cellular components, these are composed of smaller components, and this is the case all the way down to subatomic and subnuclear life, all the way to the field or Universal Mind. While spirituality states that this is actually alive and intelligent, giving life and intelligence to all higher classes of life and forms of life that it holds.

Science considers only organisms alive and nothing else. Not even the cells composing organisms are considered alive by science. While there are single cellular organisms considered by science alive, as all the microbes and bacteria, which are simple prokaryotic cells, living life independently. While the eukaryotic cells composing the human organism are more complex, as they even have a prokaryotic cell within, which is the mitochondrion, while eukaryotes are not considered by science alive.

Because if society considers human cells alive, then society has to consider the human egg alive. Which means that the human embryo is alive from conception and ever after, which means that the human embryo is a living human being since conception, which means that the embryo has human rights at all stages, which means that it has its own right to live, which means that all abortions are acts of murder, and they should be judged and punished as premeditated murder. And without abortions, all genetic lines of Earth would prosper and propagate, not only the genetic lines of those on top of society. Because there are bad people in this world committing genocide, they get away with it through Earth laws, and they get away through higher laws.

But why having these bad people in this world, mostly in our world? Can our model explain now why there are good people and bad people in this world? Why exactly does Life accept them alive, bad, and eradicating this world, when humans have worked so hard to succeed and develop, species after species, and generation after generation, for billions of years? Because there are no good people and no bad people in this world, but only people. Everybody is just the same, including those committing genocide.

Besides, these do not commit genocide, but they only allow you to kill your unborn babies yourself, and then to kill each other with chemicals, medicine, and invented terminal illnesses, to kill each other throughout wars and famines. It is also you choosing to suppress your reproductive instincts throughout your social behavior, in order to kill your own genetic line. Besides, you never get to interact with those controlling society throughout life, and therefore they never affect you in any manner, not directly, nor indirectly. They organize this entire genocide, yet since they never send the orders, they never participate in it, and this means that they are never to be blamed. Because as stated previously, those controlling society only alter the environment, in order for people to behave in the specific manner in which they destroy themselves. In the end, it will be only them alive, with the Masses and the entire Brotherhood gone, despite of what they are promised.

For supreme control and for supreme existence on Earth. Because when you study history, you learn how the Elite has always been killed throughout all wars and revolutions, and this would certainly happen with the current Elite, if the Elite do not kill the people first. And this is the law of the jungle, which is a normal behavior for any second level living being.

According to higher laws, it is not right for human beings to harass human beings, since they are of the same developmental level, and they have the same status and rights. Yet those controlling society can prove continuously that the people of Earth do not live life at the intelligent human level, since their behavior is of a very low level. And therefore, they are not humans, so they cannot have human rights.

And this is why this entire effort is done to keep people below the human level, in order to be exploited in any manner. And no matter how you study and model society along with development, human rights, existence, human origins, human behavior, and life on Earth, it always comes down to this result, human genocide, nothing more, and nothing else. And it is always done in the same manner: humans harm humans, or humans harm themselves and their children, ending up killing their own genetic line.

We have two questions here. What exactly motivates those controlling society to behave as tyrants, from a cognitive perspective, and why exactly do the people of Earth accept their control? Why can they do nothing about it even at their third intelligent developmental level?

The people of Earth behave at the third intelligent developmental level occasionally throughout life. Developmental levels are exactly modes of life, allowing you to switch them at will in order to match your needs and your meaning in life, while matching your environment. The environment of Earth is kept low artificially, while chemicals, drugs, and medicine disable the human thinking irreparably. The third intelligent developmental level is just as stable as any developmental level, allowing genuinely developed humans to protect themselves and remain on high developmental levels even indefinitely. However, developmental levels are comprehensive. You do not have to have only your reasoning at the third intelligent level, but you have to have all your abilities and characteristics at the third intelligent level, in order to remain at the third intelligent developmental level even indefinitely. When you lack only one, you decay to lower developmental levels, as you decay the rest of your abilities including your highly acclaimed reasoning. Because your responsibility has to be at the intelligent human level, along with your power to withstand this kind of attacks, along with your perception to notice this kind of attacks, along with your perseverance to protect yourself, along with your knowledge of how to protect yourself, and along with your interconnectivity with the rest of the people in order to stand together against this kind of attack. While today, people enjoy drugs and entertainment.

Why does Life accept these? Life wants the best, with the weak and the unfit to clear the way. As stated, just by reading this book, you are already at the third intelligent developmental level, at least for as long as you fulfill your third level human needs. And now, because of others who never care about fulfilling human needs, you lose. Or who knows, because more and more people seem to ascend to their intelligent human level, all seeking today this same kind of knowledge. Websites addressing higher knowledge and higher abilities come in second right after porn, while this is a great human interest, and highly promising.

Why would those controlling society engage in this dreadful behavior? It is your primal social intelligence controlling your social behavior throughout your social interaction. You as a conscious intelligence may subdue it many times, while you also end up subdued throughout your cognitive hierarchy of intelligences, throughout your various modes of life. As we see, primal intelligences do not die, but they manage to transfer themselves in an intact form from one generation to another, indefinitely. This is why I refer to them as being primal, because they are the first specialized intelligences to appear within the cognitive system of the first living being, or of the least developed living being. This means that throughout the comprehensive development of life, once primal intelligences develop, they may continue life throughout generations and throughout species at that specific level of development. From observation, you may state that current primal intelligences are of the second level at birth, having the chance to switch rapidly to the third level throughout childhood, if the family environment allows. And this is why children behave in a more competitive manner while they are little, and then they change, they develop, and you hear them wanting to become astronauts in order to colonize other planets, or to become doctors in order to cure this world, or to become presidents in order to lead this world right. These are third level intelligent human needs.

It is your social intelligence determining all your social needs, while it switches from one developmental level to another depending on the environment. Now, if you happen to be able to maintain yourself at the intelligent human level while leading an entire nation as a president, you cannot become a tyrant or a dictator, because your highly developed social intelligence along with your highly developed conscious intelligence will never allow it. However, your environment is very competitive as a president, and this may cause you to switch modes of life and drop to the second level, only to remain in power, because they will accuse you of everything only for you to resign, and lose power. You may either stay put and fight, which may cause you to drop to your second developmental level because you have to hurt others just as they hurt you, or you may choose to resign, in which case those harming you will take your place.

And with you now at the second developmental level and on top of an entire nation, you have different rules, different needs, and different responsibilities, implemented through a second level animal behavior, while all the above are also at the second level. And at the second developmental level, your social intelligence will engage you in a most competitive social fight, for one meaning, survival throughout all attacks and all fights at all costs, even if this means hurting others.

First you will defend yourself, then you will attack others before they attack you, then you attack others in order to gain their wealth and influence, and now others may find you worthy and they ally with you, they step under your authority, and then others accept your authority, only to be able to rule those below themselves in a similar dictatorial manner. An entire hierarchy of power forms in this manner, with people ruling people all the way down to the bottom social layers. You drop to the first developmental level now, and you rule for as long as this extraordinary social organism of hierarchic power allows you. Because it is so strong, that it can overtake you any time, if it did not need you for your name and for the authority and fear that you inspire.

Is it possible for you to become a dictator? No, not unless you are ready to resign first. But unlimited social power can corrupt you, so do not be too sure that you will resign. You will also behave as those controlling society today, engaging the entire human civilization in a mass genocide. Because you have to be an intelligent human being through all your abilities and characteristics, and not only through the assumed cognitive capabilities of your human mind.

And this seems a simple example, yet we have this entire model of human behavior to clarify any detail. Because you failed as a president while developed at the third level, since your nation was not entirely at the third level, with those to have attacked and challenged you winning, just because they were of lower level. And when you look around in society, it is just the same, with underdeveloped people fighting hard to obtain all leading positions, to end up controlling the most developed people today, and to end up determining them to decay, in a relatively short time. And this is how the consensual social environmental matrix is kept instated, by keeping the people underdeveloped, in every manner, indefinitely.

Yet as stated previously, humans are an exception in the wider world, since they are cognitively disabled, by lacking higher abilities. I had to add an entire level to my classification of intelligences in order to accommodate humans, the third level. Because humans were supposed to have all their highconscious cognitive abilities just as developed as the other abilities. Humans were supposed to be just as precognitive and telepathic as the rest of the mammals, while they lack these higher abilities. And if humans had these higher abilities, they never decayed, since they were capable to identify everything, and therefore they were able to defend themselves from this kind of attacks that take place at the class level of the entire civilization.

To study now those controlling society, it seems that they are also underdeveloped, while only some of their cognitive abilities are highly developed, and these include their higher powers. And now, they use their higher abilities in order to cause humans to eradicate themselves one genetic line at a time, from the bottom of society up. While they do not have to be in society to do so, they do not have to be part of the human species in order to do so, they do not have to be here on Earth in order to do so, and they do not have to be part of our world in order to do so.

Why does Life accept them? Life wants the best of the best, and this is why you see species going extinct continuously everywhere.

How can anyone lose entire abilities? Cognitive abilities as they are seen from above, are genuine intelligences as seen from within the cognitive system. And these are primal higher intelligences, as the primal emphatic intelligence, the primal telepathic intelligence, or the primal precognitive intelligence, among many others. Examples are direct manifestation, telekinesis, telepathy, and levitation, along with abilities to start fire through the power of the mind, abilities to heal directly, abilities to channel, abilities to astral project. And it seems that the entire highconscious has been removed from the brain somehow, or only the interconnection with the rest of the cognitive system has been severed, or the specific neurotransmitters allowing these cognitive abilities are absent, or the specific glands releasing these hormones and neurotransmitters are absent, disabled, or severely decayed. The last case may be true, because various hallucinogens are capable to bring back higher abilities in humans. Or this is the case only with some humans.

If you study society now, you find food additives affecting the highconscious directly, along with the entire cognitive system, removing higher abilities drastically. Fluoride does the same and it can be found in everything and not only in water. Drugs kill your higher intelligences, ideologies and social stereotypes determine you to kill them yourself, and now your higher powers are dead. And so you remain drugged and medicated strongly throughout life. While the specific hallucinogens giving you higher abilities as poorly as they do are considered very harmful drugs, and they are severely forbidden and severely punished. Capable souls who dare to come here during these times are diagnosed with autism from early childhood and they are kept heavily sedated for life. Because everything going wrong in society relates with this sustained eradication of humanity, so there is no way that humanity will find its way out from this one.

It is as wild animals coming to the zoo to persuade the captives to escape while they are still alive, because there is freedom out there, along with an independent life, along with vast wild territories and good wild food, while the captives cannot go anywhere not because they cannot see the forest or because they cannot understand freedom, but because they are in cages and cannot go anywhere. My models show the zoo one cage at a time, yet when considered as a whole, you realize that it is not exactly the human ignorance, incapability, or unwillingness to achieve an intelligent human life before they are eradicated, but it is impossible to do so, and it is too late anyway.

About our experiment with the rock on the table, we already know that the physical body is objective in nature, and if it is capable to hold an intelligence in its matrix, then we may create a living being. We already know that the intelligence is subjective in nature, so if we can only insert it in the rock, then we create life. And it does not work, it is impossible, because the physical body and the intelligences that it carries are closely interconnected.

Life, physical body, and intelligence are always together. These are facets, projections, correspondences, or perspectives of a same oneness, and cannot be taken apart. Therefore, we have to create and develop the three correspondences simultaneously, since separately it is impossible.

And this is exactly how mental models are made, since they take you through the most impossible circumstances, yet you always have to find a way to solve all problems along the way, in order to continue. Right now, we go back to Existence, since it seems to define oneness, interconnectivity, and hopefully life and intelligences. We have the existent and the nonexistent, the observed and the unobserved, and the present and the absent. Whatever we have, it relates with two opposing states, and with how they replace and succeed each other.

We may distinguish now between the present and the absent in order to begin our model, so let us do so. The rock is there on the table, and it is not there when we take it away. The rock may be intelligent or not, and therefore it may be alive or not, but at least it is existent. While it has two states, present and absent, because you can never take the rock away from existence.

So it is not a living system so far, not even a most rudimentary one, with the rock being there sometimes, and not being there other times. Besides, it is us moving the rock the entire time. Because science defines life as something animating things, or things being animated throughout life.

Which is more as a very trivial observation of what animals seem to have in common. While plants have to move in the wind in order to be considered alive by science. And this is why we have to study everything ourselves from scratch, because science never helps, mainly in the most imperative subjects as life, existence, intelligence, reality, behavior, interaction, and development.

Yet we animate the rock, we push it away, it rolls on the table, it moves, it is alive, and it is even intelligent. This is exactly zero level intelligence, which is random, monotone, or dysfunctional. And therefore, its life is of the zero level. As a reference, corporations are of the first level. Corporations exist by agreement, but they are never alive.

Maybe the rock was a bad choice, since it is not malleable enough, so we try water instead. Besides, life is mostly water, or this is what biology states. Which is observed and partially true, because life comes in many forms, not only organic, yet we try water. We place a system of pipes on the table, equipped with valves and electric pumps, in order to make the water present and not present, as fast as we can imagine. You push a button and there is water, you push the button again and the water goes away, it is not present, it went down the pipe. You may obtain the same effect by operating the valves yourself. And by having valves controlling the water throughout an entire system of pipes, you may control where the water goes and where it does not go. And therefore you may create a simple algorithmic system of intelligence, as the if-then and repeat-until system of algorithms: if you push the button there is water, while if you do not push the button, there is no water. Even more, you may have special valves that use the force of water in order to open and close themselves, and so you may encode information anywhere using binary code as it is done in computers. And it works, and you may program the water now to be there or to leave at certain times or under specific circumstances. You may even program this system of pipes to do simple math, as an abacus, and it works.

We are already at first algorithmic level of life, intelligence, and behavior, in their most rudimentary states. And now, by replacing the pipes, valves, and water, with wires, switches, and electricity, we can use digital technology, and we have just invented to laptop. We use the same first level algorithmic intelligences to create a beautiful butterfly and make it fly around the display of our laptop, and our task seems over. Or it would be over, if that insect was real. The intelligence itself may be subjective, but the body must be objectively real. And by building robots, it still does not work, since we can never get to humans by developing or evolving robots throughout time.

However, now we may study the subjective intelligence that we have created on computer. Now we know where it is, how it is created, and how it is maintained in its subjective reality. We study the hardware to see how they form a digital, informational matrix of existing and non-existing electricity throughout the switches of the motherboard. The electricity itself is objectively real, along with the wires and the entire computer hardware. Only the binary code is informational in nature, it is still part of this objective reality, yet it can form the necessary matrix that can form and hold the continuum of the subjective reality, holding now all software. And this software can be used to form computer worlds and realities, while these realities are capable to hold intelligences. And these intelligences are individual, they are not natural, and they give us the idea of what to search for in nature in order to build and evolve our human being.

What we want is something to take us to organic life, and then to real, living human beings. We want to create a model for the human being in order to be able to take it apart and study the structure and behavior of its intelligence, and then to run it in order to study its reasoning, interconnectivity, and behavior. And we already did so throughout the first two chapters, since our model of the human behavior is backwards, which means that we will achieve eventually to model a human being, even an intelligent human being.

For now, we know what we are looking for in the real

world: encoded intelligent information within entire matrices, as intelligent flickering of electricity but not chaotic flickering.

And when we look in nature, we find many examples of flickering states of observed existence. All we have to do is to look for anything allowing for the intelligent change between two states. Water or H_2O is made of two atoms of hydrogen and one of oxygen, yet this is not always the case, not with all water molecules. Study all water, to find it mostly in the H_2O state, but sometimes you find molecules of H_30, $H0$, and probably H_4O. Or probably not, yet this change from one state to another can take place in an intelligent manner, when the necessary energy is provided to change the states of water, and when these rapid successions of states of water can control this energy, and through it, can control their own state. Water can form inner, subjective realities in this manner, which can hold intelligences, and therefore which can allow life. This is a viable medium for any intelligence to project in, and to exist there as in any objective world.

Yet water has its own inner intelligence, since the field is full of intelligences. And this is how, when you are kind, you project kindness, and all snowflakes are pretty. And then when you are upset, they look chaotic and even ugly.

Or probably this is a different form of life altogether, since we are referring now to different states of water and to their intelligent fluctuation, between liquid water and ice. Because we can find these natural intelligent changes of states everywhere, and now if we are not careful, we may consider a multitude of them to represent only one form of life.

Because of Life is everywhere, in all forms of life and in all realities. Study the simplest object as a charged atom, the ion. Atoms may be charged or not, giving them two ionic states of existence necessary to form the ionic form of life. This is still digital life, with charged – not charged possibilities, yet when you have heavier elements besides hydrogen, you may have a more diverse ionic matrix, capable to hold inner intelligences. We find these ions capable to hold life everywhere, even in living beings, holding their intelligences in form of arrays.

Study cells and cellular components, to find them not exactly full of water as organic life may seem, but full of electric charge and ions, everywhere. The ATP molecules provide energy to the entire cell, but in form of charge. And this tells something, that organic life is ionic at its very base.

Flickering of ions may still be digital in nature in the case of hydrogen. The rest of charged elements may change several charges simultaneously, while they may be gathered into complex molecules that may be just as complexly charged, all flickering continuously, all capable to hold intelligences.

These intelligences are becoming more and more capable in our model. These complex intelligent flickering molecules are not digital anymore, yet they are still quantized, allowing for a form of subjective existence of a rather small cognitive resolution compared to what goes on within cells.

There is the field everywhere within cells, the gravitational and electromagnetic field, a very intense field at molecular and subcellular scales. In fact, when you study molecules and atoms, you find no particles at all, nothing material, but only field. It is at this very small scale that it becomes very tedious to distinguish between the body and the intelligence that it holds while we are searching for life, because they superimpose. And this is why the physical body and the intelligence are simple perspectives while studying life. And they should be studied together, because you cannot distinguish them one from another at nanoscopic levels and lower, which is about the smallest level that we can reach while searching for life. While at the same time, all intelligences that we have studied so far, primal or not, have their origins within living components at this small scale. And since I always suspect that there is life at levels below molecules, atoms, and nuclei, how could you ever study all these when there is nothing material, nothing tangible, nothing than the field itself, holding now matter and intelligences alike, while the most elemental intelligences that we may observe are already highly developed systems of intelligences, so developed, that they may influence life several classes of life above, all by themselves?

Yes.

Yet we found something highly important so far. We are capable now to distinguish life in all its forms and not only organic, and it is everywhere. We find it at the change of any state of the field, a change taking place in anything, while being caused by anything. The simplest system seems to be the hydrogen ion, but it is not. The simplest living system is in the field itself, since any change, any fluctuation taking place directly in the field may become a matrix of life capable to hold inner realities and therefore intelligences. There are two very distinguishable states in the field: the electric and the magnetic states, constantly fluctuating one into another under specific circumstances. These are the main interchanging states found in everything, triggered by everything, and capable to hold matrices, continuums, inner realities, and within inner realities, capable to hold intelligences. You may have intelligences and therefore intelligent life directly in the field, directly in the void. And there we may find individual intelligences in theory, within the faintest fluctuations of the field, fluctuations coming in form of standing electromagnetic or gravitational oscillations taking place around any point of equilibrium within the field. These are the elemental intelligences that we are seeking, which are formed and maintained continuously throughout this world, having their roots right in the raw field, or in the Universal Mind as spirituality calls it.

And we have finally found our individual intelligence to start our model for the human being, and through it, for the human behavior. Because now we may find the specific manners in which cellular components are capable to draw intelligence and therefore life from the field itself, by triggering these specific vibrations between the electric and the magnetic sides or states of the field in specific manners, in order to form inner realities with larger intelligences. These unite to form the cellular intelligence, and through it, the cellular life. Furthermore, these form organisms, primal intelligences, along with reasoning, needs, behavior, human environment.

Since the field is at the base of matter and electromagnetic radiation throughout this world, everything is formed by the field, everything lays in the field, while everything in this world has at the base matter, along with these elemental intelligences found at each point in the universe, continuously oscillating or vibrating around their state of equilibrium. While this is the Law of Vibration, making Life and Intelligence possible.

You might not be able to harvest energy from elemental intelligences, yet you may employ them throughout computers, since they offer a way out for digital and quantum computer technology, toward continuous, analogue informational platforms capable to offer a very high informational resolution, along with a direct interface with the human brain. And you may do so by employing high-density field instead of wires and switches. Or you may clone directly brain tissue in very large pools, and if you know how to teach it, you have your intuitive or even your intelligent supercomputer. If you clone cortex tissue.

As another remark, all these elemental intelligences may unite to form a comprehensive intelligence or system of intelligences capable to span the One. And this is the interconnective matrix capable to model any interconnectivity between intelligences. This has spiritual meanings, while offering a way toward the highconscious intelligence and its continuous interconnection with the Universal Mind.

Ionic life is based on the intelligent ionic vibration, ionic matrix capable to change the field around, and capable to be changed by the field around. Through the field, we notice a form of interconnectivity among the most elemental forms of intelligences. Vibrating ions modify the field around, while the field modifies other ions, keeping in this manner an entire living system vibrating and interconnected.

We have found the base of organic life, and it is ionic in nature. While the base of ionic life has the standing oscillations taking place around points of equilibrium found at any point and moment of the field. And now, once we are here, we may find our way through development, all the way up to living human beings.

And again, it does not matter what higher cognitive activity takes place at the moment, a common daydream or an intense analytical cognitive reasoning, since these kind of worlds have to manifest and succeed continuously throughout all realities, all the way to the One, and most importantly, all being relatively similar to what takes place at the level of the One itself, only progressively decomposed cognitively down the existential line of repeatedly created realities.

Everything going on here in this world, all people, all information, all laws of physics, everything takes place according to our higher reality. This entire model of the human behavior relates to and addresses our higher reality directly, and not our world, since our world is only a fragment of it, it is only as much and as long it is needed for a mental model to take place and reach its intended result, the final solution. And then you wake up in another dream, and you do so all over again, you behave normally and consistently to your new scene, to your new fragment of the outer reality, undergoing your behavior toward finding the successful solution that the higher world demands.

And this is exactly why everything around is consistent to an infinite universe, filled with stars, galaxies, and with zillions of living beings and events taking place everywhere. While in fact, you may be here in our world for a limited time, along with a limited number of beings, in this instantaneous, fragmentary world, where everything is but a stage, a simulation.

While the same actors participate in all mental models, with only the stage or scenery changing according to the setting in the higher world. These actors are genuine living beings and they may transcend and project from world to world following their models, plays, and simulations, as needed, and probably even according to their own needs, interests, and abilities. And this is how, seen from the perspective of the One, you have specific mental models taking place in the most adequate replicas of this world, from the most adequate worlds and realities, simulated by the most adequate intelligences, according to their needs, abilities, and interests. And this is how you have the best of the best ever, in what it concerns higher reasoning at the supreme level of the One.

Yet this is the case only if this world is created naturally, as part of a natural, higher cognitive system, the Universal Mind. Because this world may be created artificially, as by a higher computer, similar to your videogames. Or this world may be created naturally, in a higher mind, yet being not a mental model used throughout higher reasoning, but being a daydream, used for joy, thrill, and socialization. All records and testimonies point to this specific model for the existence of our world, and we should consider it in details.

Note that we skip the big bang theory. The universe is infinite, but only as it seems. Because this world, if it is created, then it may have its borders anywhere, in the lower orbit of Earth, as many claim, or further out in space, or down to the surface of Earth, with only your continent to be real, while the rest of this world is only claimed to be there, while it is not. Anything may be the case with created realities, while all records and testimonies state that this world is created, either naturally, or artificially.

What we know so far is that regardless of our assumption, all our knowledge and understanding here in this world, including all these models, address only the higher reality and they benefit the higher reality. Because I used facts found directly in this world, while this world is a replica of our higher reality. While all these facts were placed here in our world with the intention to serve throughout mental models, with all results benefiting the higher reality.

What millions of witnesses state is that when they die, they reunite with their loved ones, and then they either return to this world together, in order to live another lifetime, this time under slightly different circumstances, or they go elsewhere, to other realities, to live there. But not too many do, so they stay around here. It seems that they are the souls, and they choose where they want to go and what reality to live in. And when they do so, they live entire lives there. What is important to state is that souls live successions of lifetimes within specific worlds and circumstances, in order to understand minutely these events and circumstances, from all angles and perspectives. These are the true actors performing all mental models, higher and lower, they go from one world to another, higher and lower, to choose their subjects and settings according to their higher needs, sent to them directly by Life and by Intelligence, which are the supreme perspectives of the One. And this is how souls digest cognitively various circumstances throughout the One, down to cognitive elements. While you are one of them, and you do the same right now, alongside your loved ones accompanying you everywhere you go.

What we want now is to know exactly how everything is possible, how these worlds and replicas of this worlds are formed, who these actors are, what they are doing everywhere, and how exactly they get there. Yet we have answered these questions and more, throughout our model. All realities are the same, and they are similar to our world. All intelligences are similar, even while you are one of them, while all worlds and replicas of this worlds are created in the exact manner in which you have created yours. Yet what you do not know due to your lack of higher abilities here in this world is how telepaths form common replicas of this world together, and how they reason and daydream there together. And even more, when they follow their natural needs closely, telepaths reason in form of common daydreams.

What would you do if you were a telepath? Steal the answers to all your tests from your colleagues? Find out the best kept secrets of all your friends? Become a detective and start investigating crimes? Well, not really. What you would do most of the time, you would probably get into people's minds in order to follow their lives and daydreams, because they are better than movies. Or this is what you would do if you were alone. Because when you are a telepath, around dozens of telepaths, you daydream together, and it is extraordinarily beautiful, better than real life. It is as watching movies that you create yourself in any manner you please, while helped by others, all daydreaming alongside you. And with hundreds or thousands of telepaths daydreaming together, you may have larger worlds as this world, where you may do anything you please. This is what animals do while hibernating, if they still have their higher powers. This is what cats do while purring, since the sound helps them interconnect with each other, while helping them entrain their own brainwaves.

And now, within entire worlds of telepaths, they are involved in creating worlds as this one, where they live normal lives together in a safe and relatively fast manner. Yet what you may want is not to remember who you are in your real world, for a better experience. And so you have this world we call Earth, with everything happening here good and bad, being equally enjoyable for these higher beings.

Or this is the case with part of the people of Earth, because the other part may be imaginarily created in order to fit various meanings. And now, among all models of this world, this one fits the most all historic, mythological, religious, and spiritual records, along with millions of testimonies from people who had the chance to go in and out of this world.

Yet life is not so safe and pleasant even by living it virtually within collectively imagined realities, because there are people and intelligences seeking to profit of everything, including you and your loved ones, and these are everywhere, in all realities, higher and lower. They can rob you, replace you, disable you, exploit you, use you, subdue you, and lure you into confined realities by promising you everything, even that they are the holly promised realities.

Where exactly is the joy in these created violent worlds? Who exactly would want to live there? Where exactly is the joy? And even more, who would ever create bad people that will turn around to harass and harm even you, their creator? Nobody wants bad people around them, along with bad events happening to them.

Or at least this is always the case in your own objectively real world. Because in your daydream, you may have anything you choose, even violent dreams. It is as playing videogames, because nobody plays the good, safe, beautiful ones, but only the rough, bad, violent, challenging ones. And the more menacing they are, the more you want to play them. Because you are bad, very bad, or this is how society labels you, and this is how you consider yourself, which might not be true. It is an extraordinary opportunity that you have to follow your needs closely, and play all violent games that you find and enjoy. Because as an actor within the universal mind, it is you choosing your role within your mental models, along with your settings, worlds, and realities, according to your needs, interests, abilities, and means.

And you are never alone doing so, because through you, your soul becomes involved in your videogame, along with its soul, and its soul's soul. They learn survival skills and strategy thinking from you, and it is highly important. Because if you do not have these skills, then you can never withstand attacks, and look at what happens to the human civilization.

Yet this world is not bad entirely, but mostly good and civilized, everywhere, with problems and successes, along with unlimited opportunities to learn and develop everywhere. While you always become involved in them, you always seek all chances that you have to get in trouble or to explore new territories. You still get in trouble eventually, then it takes you some time to find your way out, and this is life. And in the end, what you are left with are not exactly beautiful butterflies that you play with in a beautiful summer day, but what you are left with are these experiences, good and bad, everything to have taught you something this life, otherwise you lived an entire life in vain.

And if you never have these experiences good and bad, well then, you have to watch TV, surf the Net, or play videogames, and it might be similar to real life. Or you may do so if you do not get bored. Because if you still get bored, then you do not fulfill your meaning, yet. This does not mean that you have to start playing war videogames immediately, or engage in acts of violence. Because these are examples of second level extreme animal behavior, while you are a third level intelligent living human being. And if you still get bored regardless of how intense these become, then you were supposed to become engaged in third level intelligent human activities, as studying, performing art, or writing books. Try these, and if you do not get bored now, then seek a variety of third level activities, while also seeking to pinpoint your exact third level need, because that is your meaning in life. You have to follow your needs closely, yet do so in a manner in which you do not harm others, since genuinely developed humans engage only in win-win circumstances, and they never harm living beings. And if you are right here and right now in these specific times of this world, you might be here to test your capabilities to be able to develop to your true potential under the most unfavorable conditions, or to truly develop to the intelligent human level, since this is exactly what you and your higher self need to do and desire. And this might be why you read this book.

To return to our model of the human being now, we study how specific molecules called amino acids can interact with the field better than individual ions. These are complex in charge distribution, and now when they vibrate in the overall cellular field, they are capable to influence the field in a more diverse manner, allowing the formation of genuine inner realities capable to hold intelligences within. And with amino acids forming proteins, we find now one of the most extended ways of forming inner realities and intelligences, proteins. All these charged structures are considered alive, since they have both a body and an intelligence. And this includes ions, amino acids, and now proteins, along with enzymes and steroids. Individually, these may hold easily evolved algorithmic life of the first level, while when interconnected in arrays, they are capable to form wider, more capable intelligences of the second developmental level, capable of intuitive thinking. And these are exactly your current primal intelligences, this is when and how they were formed, and they are still alive today, right there in your cognitive system.

For example, your reproductive intelligence will still go out of your body through arrays of steroids, proteins, amino acids, and ions, in order to tend to all its tasks not in your own organism, but throughout the organisms of those around. Mothers know when to feed babies, through these reproductive intelligences that go out of their own organism in order to tend to the young ones. Pheromones will enter the bodies of your perspective mates in order to determine them to choose you, while all these behaviors are intuitive, or they are probably even of the third level, capable of reasoning.

As we see, ions, amino acids, and proteins may not have to live within cells, but they may live independently, outside cells, since this is the normal molecular form of life. What characterizes organic life is that it tends to accumulate its developmental achievements one on top of another. They do not always discard the old structures, but they let them accumulate one on top of another throughout the development of the physical body, or they include them within newer, better structures.

For example, your pineal gland is nothing but the first eye ever developed, as a mean of distinguishing between light and darkness. This eye had neurons developing all around it for every cognitive task involving the inner and outside world, until it ended up right in the middle of the brain. It cannot see anything anymore, yet it is still there, as a gland producing hormones. And where there are hormones, these hold an intelligence, and this is a primal higher intelligence. Now study the axis of hormones to understand all cognitive hierarchies of intelligences that it forms and controls, throughout what modes of life and for what reasons, to find it controlling the cognitive system and the organism throughout its higher behavior and developmental behavior, including the cognitive development.

Cells are different than organisms, since cells do not develop as much as organisms do. Yet not even the development of organisms is as spectacular as it may seem, because the entire development from one species to another consists of various manners of arranging trillions of cells together, in the best shape, in order to match an ever-changing environment, and nothing else. It is just as arranging the pillows on your sofa in the most convenient manner to match the shape of your back, and nothing else. While the pillows or cells never change themselves.

What we may do regarding cells is to go back in time in order to see how they were formed, and how their cellular components became what they still are today within cells.

We may study in this manner all cellular components, in order to find out when, how, and why specific improvements have been introduced. The transition from ions to amino acids and then to proteins, enzymes, and steroids has been made gradually, with the intention of interacting with the field in a more diverse manner, now through a more complex charge distribution. And if you vary this charge as needed, while oscillating it around in the field in various manners, you may create a field matrix around, necessary for holding inner realities at higher informational resolution. You need energy and charge coming from the outside in the process, and you may take these easily from the surrounding chemical elements, if you only know how to bring them together and make them interact. What you do as a protein, you may vary the field around in order to bring chemical compounds close enough together to make them react, and then you may harvest the energy and ions resulting from this reaction in order to modify your own movement in the field along with your charge distribution. Or you may swallow compounds wholly, in specific orders, to allow them to react within yourself, or to allow them to react with parts of yourself, harvesting all resulting energy and charge. This may be hard, mostly when you are only dozens or hundreds of times bigger than the reacting compounds giving you charge and energy. But as an entire array of similar proteins, you may fulfill your task easily. And we notice now the birth of the first primal eating intelligence, since it used chemosynthesis at first.

Through arrays of proteins, you are capable to hold a larger, smarter system of intelligences, while you are more powerful.

And this is how classes of life of a larger level are preferred over individual living beings, even at the protein level.

Note that proteins do not have to live within cells. As arrays, proteins live in higher classes of life, and they may live anywhere. All that they need is a soup of chemical compounds all around, as it can be found in the water around volcanoes today.

These arrays of proteins do not need only energy and charge in order to keep them alive, but they have to replicate themselves. Arrays of proteins are capable to bring amino acids together through their own field, in order to form new proteins. This is a different task than feeding, since you have to modify the field in a specific manner in order to form new proteins, in contrast with harvesting energy and charge from reacting compounds. And this is how you have specialization along with interconnected community life within groups of proteins living together.

We are further enough in time to distinguish how this specialization took place. How exactly do proteins know what they need and what they do not need in order to cope with the environment? How exactly do antelopes know how to modify and develop their hoofs and legs in order to make them the most capable at running through tall grass several thousands of years down the road? Or a better question here is how species know how to evolve in order to cope with their environment. And another question is how does the bottom of the puddle know how to match the hole in the road. We must ask evolution, since evolution claims ownership over all knowledge related to development. Yet evolution states only one thing, that species evolve. Nothing more, nothing less. The later theory called survival of the fittest, states that species either evolve or die, and so the species to have evolved so far never died, and therefore they are still around. How trivial.

We are going to see how living beings never develop in order to cope with the environment or else they die, but they develop as a natural integration in the environment, matching it in all its details. The difference is very slight, and we lacked the proper setting in order to state it when we found the cyclical lifeline of causality regarding developmental behavior, in the first chapter. Let us see.

We may claim now that all intelligences held by arrays of proteins managed to specialize and therefore develop to their current specialization or ability within the community, through cyclical, repeated developmental behavior, through trial and error, yet this might have not been the case. Because the environment at that very small scale is different than the tall grass, waves, and beaches that we are familiar with in the macro world.

Down at very small scales, the field is so significant, that you are not capable to distinguish intelligences from the bodies that carry them. And then when these individuals vibrate and change charges, the entire field changes, entraining everything around. There is strong motion everywhere, continuously changing, attracting, and repelling, moving you everywhere. But most importantly, there are intelligences everywhere, both in the micro world and macro world. The environment is full of them, since the environment is never void of life, science states, but it is full of life, and everything is intelligent. It is not chaotic at all but ordered and alive, since similar proteins are everywhere around, and you have to share every corner of the field with them, every motion that it makes, you share everything. And now, in this crowded environment, everything that you want to do and achieve, or any manner in which you want to develop, is right there, in the field, and you know everything.

Therefore, it is not a question of you learning to cope with the environment throughout a cyclical lifeline of trial and error, but it is a matter of you having the opportunity to expand your behavior in order to accumulate another free gap in the field, another free place, another free specialization, another niche element of the field, or an entire other niche. Because if there is a small field oscillation available at the proximity of your existence, then you are the first to spread out to take it, a good opportunity. You do not work hard to cope with the environment or you die, you lost, and now the entire world pushes you out of existence, but you take your opportunity to influence the field a little stronger, a little longer, with each little opportunity that you have. Because the field is full of intelligences as it is, all intelligences being unique and involved in harmony or competition for this unique identity. And with each random opportunity that you have in order to expand and influence the field better and in a unique manner, then you manage to keep and define your identity among the rest of intelligences. Development is not a continuous struggle to cope with the environment, but an opportunity for uniqueness, and for a larger niche. You integrate continuously within your changing environment as an opportunity, by matching the changing environment with your behavior, and not exactly by modifying your behavior in a challenging environment.

This seems to be a difference in words, yet when you place it on your lifeline of causality, you notice that two relevant elements regarding evolution switch places within the lifeline of causality, with your behavior causing you to integrate in the environment and not with the environment causing you to integrate in the environment.

Again, in other words, you adapt to the environment exactly at the moment the change in the environment takes place, and you do so naturally, as an integration in the environment rather than as an adaptation to the environment. Because you adapt to the environment before the change in the environment takes place, and then when it does, you simply match your environment. Or this is the case for reoccurring changes. Which means that the environment is harmonious in all instances and details, accepting you in its harmony just as well.

And this answers the riddle with the puddle and the hole in the road, because it is never a matter of continuous struggle to carve every single detail in the puddle to match the hole in the road, but it is harmony at all levels and from all perspectives everywhere, from the nanoscopic level of ionic intelligences, to Life herself, and this includes our puddle in the road, along with the human behavior, this entire world, and probably the Consensual Matrix, or not.

How does it take place? You follow all your developmental needs, and they take you there. This is possible under specific environments, when the environment is filled with instances and outcomes and you are forced to take what you get, any change in the environment, and you become that specialized intelligence from then on, as an opportunistic outcome. And this is possible through mental models predicting future events, capable to be very precise in predicting environments already filled with events, since there are not many left.

Yet we should state here that both possibilities are true, since you work hard and fight in order to cope with the environment continuously throughout life if you happen to be at the second developmental level and lower, because if you are at the third developmental level, you maintain the harmony everywhere within your environment, and therefore you integrate yourself perfectly in the environment, matching it minutely, with the environment integrating around you, matching you similarly. And this is the case because environments are not void of life and intelligence, but they are full of life and intelligence, many times matching your own behavioral level.

We have modeled so far the eating intelligence and the reproductive intelligence as they were born billions of years ago. Another significant primal intelligence of those times is the excretion intelligence. This intelligence used its field to repel and move away any unwanted molecules from the protein community. Another cellular structure of reference is the cellular membrane, to appear over one billion years ago. These dates match what science states, yet the dates themselves have little significance for our model, since only their order matters. What happens is that the environment changed suddenly then, filling up with oxygen from excessive photosynthesis. Oxygen is highly corrosive, and it harmed proteins and protein communities. One type of protein array in the community expanded to place itself as a shield of force against anything coming in, managing to protect the initial environment of the community. With a cellular membrane, supplies still had to get in the cell, while waste had to go out. It is the job or opportunity of a newly specialized intelligence to let the goods in and send the waste out. This specific intelligence became therefore specialized with the interaction of the entire cell with the outside world, intelligence residing directly in the cellular membrane. This specific primal intelligence became the conscious cellular intelligence, and it is now you.

Intelligences do not reside somewhere in their physical body, but they span entirely the body. Whatever shape it has, the body does not exactly hold intelligences, but the body is the correspondent counterpart that intelligences are in this real world. The body may not be exactly in the shape of intelligences since physical bodies hold intelligences in a matrix, while the matrix is held and maintained by the body entirely. Yet the body might be identical with what intelligences perceive themselves to be outside and within their own inner world. It is the same with your inner self and your physical body from the outside world, since your inner self is exactly in the shape of your physical body from the outside world. And this is how bodies are what intelligences are in their inner world, and vice versa. Since this is the supreme characteristic of correspondence of Life, or the Supreme Law or Correspondence of Life.

There is one important difference in this statement. Your inner self is not as your body from the outside world, but it is exactly how you see your body in the outside world through your senses of perception and understanding. Because your eyes do not see the word as it is, since your eyes distort the image in several manners in order to distinguish everything of importance in the outside world. Because this world outside is gray and blurry, with all colors and details mixed and scrambled. You have a lens in your eyes to clear the details and project their image on the retina, while you have photoreceptors in form of cones in the retina, acting as prisms, used now to split apart light into the multitude of distinct colors, assigning in this manner unique colors to all shapes and details, to define your familiar objects and people exactly as you see them. While these look different in the real world, since they are undistinguishable there.

Therefore, not only that you are different in your inner replica of this world than in the outside world, but your entire inner replica of this world is significantly different than the outside world. And since your added understanding and association makes your inner replica of this world more comprehensible, everything is meant to facilitate reasoning in a most efficient manner.

As we have already seen, your inner replica of this world is a digested form of the outside world made in your image, while your own inner intelligences take your inner word to digest it cognitively further, according to your analytical thinking and mental models, with further inner intelligences digesting it even further, down to basic algorithms.

To return to the cellular membrane now, you find it made of various charged molecules, resembling more to a wall made of plasma. This entire charged membrane moves and waves continuously, as it interacts with the field in order to maintain its intelligence in its subjective reality along with its conscious replica of the outside and inside environments of the cell.

This is how, when cellular membranes started to surround communities of proteins, ions, amino acids, RNA, and arrays of these, these individual living beings had a similar lifestyle and behavior before and after the cellular membrane. Cells interacted with the outside world as a whole, and became more capable, stronger, and more powerful, yet still cooperating with free arrays of proteins and with various other cells from the outside world, undertaking new specializations.

And this is how intelligences lived, many times indefinitely. Because intelligences formed by individual proteins died alongside their physical bodies, while the larger intelligences held by arrays of proteins lived longer or indefinitely, by being able to replace gradually their dead proteins from their array, with new ones.

Through specialization and by having a cellular wall, the environment within the cell became secure and relatively abundant. This allowed a constant environment along with predictable outcomes in all domains, with small exceptions. This stopped the cellular development, yet at the level of simplicity of proteins, there is little or no room for physical improvement and therefore for development, since any change interferes with the simple laws of physics, chemistry, and electrodynamics. This is why communities of proteins could not adapt to the drastic change in the environment, because you cannot change the shapes and components of molecules or you destroy them, so they had to preserve the environment around themselves by wrapping the membrane around the entire community.

The cellular membrane developed continuously while integrating in its outside environment, while the cellular components remained the same. Later on, eukaryotes appeared as new, larger cellular communities, wrapping around the wider community another membrane meant to include entire cells, arrays, and individual living beings. The common double stranded DNA appeared as a method to preserve information by storing it in two different forms linked together in the form of a ladder. Each strand contains the same information, in form of RNA, linked one to another, RNA consisting of prototype proteins linked one to another, for better preservation.

It is significant to model here the cellular behavior. You may compare cells with social communities or with organisms composed of cells, yet you cannot compare their behaviors. If individuals of an organism or society are born, learn, grow up, and then take their job in the organism or community, proteins are replicated and they are ready to take over their specialization right away, since through their specific movement, shape, and charge distribution, they are capable to interact with the field in the specific manner that it is needed for performing their task. When the job is no longer needed, then no more proteins are replicated.

This model compares proteins with little robots, while proteins are alive and intelligent. However, the intelligence that proteins carry is algorithmic in nature, and with all bodies almost identical, all protein intelligences are almost identical. The overall larger intelligences that they form as an array are more capable, and are of the second intuitive level. While this is the basic molecular form of life, with viruses as an example.

When eukaryotes appeared and formed organisms, they made and organized the entire organism in their own image, since these organisms as a whole were meant to occupy similar niches, while undergoing similar behaviors as individual cells once did. It was only an increase in the class level, it happened before from ions to amino acids, then from amino acids to proteins, then from proteins to cells or communities of protein arrays, and then from prokaryotes to eukaryotes, now to organisms of eukaryotes, and to communities of organisms. Regardless of the increase in the level of class of life, cells and cellular components never changed, while creating specialized systems within organisms to function in the image, behavior, and niche once occupied by the protein arrays and the primal intelligences occupying them. You may still see these arrays of proteins spreading everywhere to span the organism, as hormones, or exiting the organism as pheromones. While the conscious intelligence of the cellular membrane became the skin of the organism, still tending to the interaction of the entire organism with the outside world. Later on, when the organism needed a more capable cognitive system, they made a specialized thinking organ out of skin, and folded it up into a brain. And then further on, for humans, they added even more skin on top of the brain, in order to be able to perform new intelligent conceptual cognitive tasks. And this is how you have developed from a cellular membrane to skin, to a brain, and then to a cortex.

But who exactly does these major transformations from one species to another? Is there a primal intelligence specialized in the development of the entire species? There are primal developmental intelligences for the entire cell and the entire organism, while all intelligences and primal intelligences maintain their old specializations or learn to develop in order to occupy newer ones. And only if their specific environmental condition that they tend to changes progressively, then they develop progressively accordingly, and this may be seen as a continuous development.

What primal intelligences do, they figure out what is wrong with them when the environment changes, and they solve these new problems within their cognitive replica of this world. They solve these new environmental problems in an objective manner there, by modifying the existing components of the replica of this world, and by transporting them anywhere needed. Within your own replica of this world, everything is a simple or complex memory or information, which are intelligences. In the case of development of entire species, primal intelligences move intelligences around their cognitive world, or they move around intelligences within these intelligences in order to change their shape, while the outside body changes accordingly, because the body is only the real image of the inner cognitive world where intelligences live. And this is how physical development is simply an immediate consequence of the development of the cognitive world where primal intelligences live. And since through their continuous mental models, primal intelligences live in the future throughout their mental models that they enact themselves, and they are capable to make all changes and adaptations of the physical body in time, for all changes in the environment to occur dozens, hundreds, or thousands of years ahead. And they can predict the changes in the environment because they already have the environment replicated in their cognitive worlds, while all changes already take place within their environment well in advance, according to their mental models.

Which means that species do not develop comprehensively in a probabilistic manner, with the capable species surviving drastic changes in the environment and with the less fortunate incapable unsuccessful species dying away, but all species, all living beings, all primal intelligences, all developmental intelligences, and in general all cellular intelligences are capable to predict and cope with the entire environment in a normal intuitive intelligent manner. Even mental models are coordinated in an intuitive intelligent manner, and now exactly probabilistically by chance, with the random unsuccessful mental models scrapped away, and with the successful random mental models generating random successful ideas. Because as always seen, randomness is only the zero level of cognition, behavior, development, and subsistence, as Life starts with the second intuitive level.

There is more to consider, since all animals within a species are interconnected, while they have similar cognitive replicas of this world, always striving to find solutions to all problems even before they happen. These replicas of this world and mental models may be interconnected in any manner, through the field or through messenger proteins, and so species exchange information.

And information is exchanged among members of a same species, because of one major issue, genetic decay. By exchanging information, members of a same species compare all information within the DNA, while keeping in all organisms a homogenized version of all DNA found within all organisms of the species. And this is how the most common adaptation to the environment remains in this most homogenized DNA sequence. DNA is not a blueprint, but a physical storage of all protein prototypes, as linked strings of RNA. And if you are searching for information within the DNA, you find it inside the prototype proteins, held in there as intelligences, along with their normal replicas of this world, normal changes in the organism to have always taken place, along with all intelligences, primal and inner, along with the entire cognitive system, which contains now this entire developmental information, stocked up one on top of another, prototype after prototype.

Therefore, with each change in the physical appearance of

the species, this specific change has to make it first within these prototype proteins stored in the DNA, and then these changes appear in the offspring, years and decades later, hopefully just in time for the environmental changes.

What changes? There are major ages of ice-water-drought taking place on Earth every twenty-five thousand years or so, due to a cyclical movement of the axis or Earth called precession. During precession, ice melts, global water rises over one hundred meters, and this is how what was covered by ice once becomes proper land now, while what was proper land once is covered by water now. Entire niches are displaced many times thousands of kilometers, temperatures change, oxygen levels fluctuate, this allows trees to change in size, animals change in size, and furs become shorter or longer. Luckily, these changes are cyclical, and species are able to recycle old adaptations for the new conditions. When these environmental changes are gradual, as it is the case through precession, species have the necessary time to predict and adapt. Yet many times, drastic changes in the environment happen suddenly, as in cataclysms involving super volcanoes, asteroids, solar flares, and polar shifts. Under these drastic, sudden circumstances, species shrink in number and die, creating throughout Earth an entire range of new, unoccupied niches, since the old niches are no more.

And this is how new species appear relatively fast, to occupy the new niches. Because within species that are small in numbers, it is easy for all adaptations to make it in the DNA of the entire species, and the entire species changes in shape and details significantly, sometimes exiting the class entirely if the earth environment changes too drastically. It happened over sixty million years ago, when the environment changed so much, that two new classes appeared simultaneously, the birds, and the mammals.

Yet there is more than DNA transmitted from one generation to another. To model it, we have to return to cells and follow their division. Cells are modeled as individual beings by biology, yet cells are not individual beings, but communities of individual living beings, surrounded by a membrane. Through division, cellular communities split in two, with each daughter cell keeping a similar number of cellular community members. This is how these arrays of proteins end up intact in both cells after division, keeping their primal intelligences intact, after having duplicated themselves. These are the same cellular intelligences to have remained alive for billions of years. And this is the case because intelligences are not individual living beings, but they are cognitive communities of other intelligences. It is similar with cells, since cells are communities of individual cellular components. And now, when communities divide, entire samples of the previous community may carry on, grow up, develop, and regain their initial size, capabilities, and tasks, while the cellular community in itself remains just as it was before division.

And now, during the reproduction of the entire organism, there are entire samples of cellular communities and therefore of cognitive systems sent to become the new organism, samples growing naturally, while reconstructing the parent organisms, as colonies. Ending up reconstructing the old civilization. And with samples of all primal intelligences being transferred to the new generation at the moment of conception, all primal intelligences never actually die, as they are never born, but they are only sampled and replanted elsewhere.

You the conscious intelligence are as old as organic life, and a lot older, since you have your roots in ionic life, and before that, in subatomic and subnuclear life, and before that, in the raw field or Universal Mind, and you have been carried intact through these various life forms, classes of life, species, races, and countless of succeeding generations of individuals, in your exact initial form, with the rest of living structures added to you throughout development. You were an array of proteins, becoming a cellular membrane, then taken entirely as a whole to become a skin of an organism, then being transferred wholly to become part of a nervous system, then part of a brain, and then part of a cortex. With you always inside the cells, to have been always transferred throughout division, while always performing these same tasks of a conscious intelligence.

It is the same with your primal intelligences, since throughout billions of years, they fed you, recovered you, helped you interact socially, they reproduced you, and here you are now, a living human being, the most capable organism and cognitive system in the known universe.

How exactly do you reproduce? Easy to answer. But how does the organism reproduce and how does it know exactly how to grow and become exactly what its parents used to be, do, and look? There is the DNA sequence of information, constituting the blueprint for all these, or this is what you assume. While the DNA sequence has the prototypes of cellular components as proteins, along with instructions of what to do with these and when to do so, and nothing more. We refer to these as proteins in the outside world, but in their own cognitive world, these are intelligences.

In other words, the DNA does not contain all the needed information to make an entire living human organism from scratch, as the current science states in ignorance, but the DNA contains all the necessary specialized prototype intelligences who know well how to perform all the specialized tasks needed to develop the entire living human organism throughout gestation and later on throughout life, while assuring the necessary survival, subsistence, and further development while fulfilling Life and the wider world in everything that it does. These specialized prototype protein intelligences are transferred intact from one generation to another through DNA, while all instructions of how to handle the DNA are also specialized intelligences.

One of these instructions is how to take one of those eukaryotic cells from the beginning of our model, and develop it through all classes, species, races, and individuals, generation after generation, to grow it up now and make it look just like the parents. And this is the case because cells and organisms always develop by adding new changes or adaptations of all kind on top of the old ones. This is how, after each conception, each egg becomes the original eukaryote. Then it grows to become the multicellular organism of the first species, then it undergoes all changes throughout that species, then it becomes the second species, then all changes of that species, until it is born. Then it grows up, and then, at maturity, it ends up to look just as its parents. The egg does not actually develop to become an adult, biology states, but the egg follows the entire development of the entire organic life since the first cell, billions of years ago. And now you notice the correspondent resemblance between behavior and development. Or between Life and development.

Did humans really come from apes? Can you see the smooth transition from apes directly to humans? Probably yeti, snowman, bigfoot, and the sasquatch came from apes, because when you study the human embryo throughout gestation, you may find other species succeeding right before birth. And these last species that humans used to be not too long ago used to be psychic in nature and highly capable. And to make matters more relevant, embryos in the very last stage of gestation look similar to the humans currently inhabiting the vast areas found toward the middle of our galaxy, with larger heads, larger eyes, and smaller mouths. And now a large part of your behavior used to be part of their behavior, since your primal intelligences used to be part of their intelligences, intact. You used to be them, not too long ago, and therefore you do what they did, not too long ago. And you probably seek to have your environmental conditions at the level that it was back then, offering you the higher knowledge and higher abilities that you had back then. All these significant details have to be part of the model of the human being, and therefore part of the model of the human behavior.

Why having to go through all forms of life and species, all over again during gestation? Simply because cellular intelligences never die, but they only improve and develop. And with each conception, they send samples of themselves to become the new cognitive system, which is in fact the old one exactly, as it had gone through everything that the old cognitive system did. There are no blueprints for life in the DNA, since these are impossible to be made by intelligences and use. Because life is very complex, and as I always state, living beings and their intelligences are larger and more complex than entire worlds and realities.

And now you understand how important is for human beings to behave successfully, because if they fail, these extraordinary primal intelligences measuring their age in billions of years, suddenly die. And this is why they push you in every way to succeed in everything, develop and reproduce, in order for them to remain alive, through your descendants. And this is why those controlling society want you and your genetic line out of the way unless you are one of them, because these billion-year-old intelligences have been harmonious with each other in every manner and have been successful this entire time, until you.

The End

This book series continues with the next book, "Flat Earth." Here is a short synopsis:
Is the Earth flat or spherical? There is only one way to find out the truth. Just go up there in the orbit of Earth, see it for yourself, and then come back to tell us the story. You may always rely on everything that others claim, officially or not, that the Earth is flat or spherical, but when all their statements and proofs remain inconclusive, since they did not go up there in the orbit of Earth to see it themselves, regardless of what they may claim, you have to keep searching.
Yet when you study the current science with all its space missions and space records, even these remain inconclusive, as though space missions have never reached past the lower orbit of Earth themselves. Therefore, now we have additional important questions to ask, besides those regarding the true shape of Earth. Is there anything at all past the lower orbit of Earth? No, according to all space records, regardless of what

science may claim.

Because as long as you cannot go past the lower orbit of Earth as an individual or as an entire valid space mission to see everything yourself, and as long as the current science remains incapable to provide the necessary scientific evidence stating that the Earth is spherical and that our world spans past the lower orbit of Earth as we see in the sky, then everyone, the entire humanity remains incapable to prove that Earth is flat or spherical. Since just as all flatearthers and planoterrestrials out there struggle to prove that the Earth is flat, now you have the entire science, with its entire army of millions of employed scientists incapable to prove that Earth is spherical and that there is anything out there past the lower orbit of Earth.

Because this unique circumstance questions not only the accurate shape of Earth, not only the pertinence and reliability of the current science, but it questions the meaning and nature of this entire world. And if you are only starting your search for truth right now, to see if Earth could be flat and not spherical, there is significantly more going on than contorted science and fake space missions, while you should research harder to find out truth.

Because you cannot simply solve a mathematical equation here at the surface of Earth to find out its shape and nature, while you cannot rely on science to tell you the truth as it lies persistently, and now you have to figure out everything on your own.

Yet there are still ways to tell if Earth is spherical of flat, by the laws of physics here at the surface of Earth matching space objects or flat surfaces, or matching rotating objects or stationary ones, as we will see shortly in the book.

Yet you always have to be careful throughout your studies, because many times, created realities are made with the main intention to seem larger and therefore more credible, fooling you the entire time. While dreams and videogames do just the same. And therefore, now you have to consider these details just as well, along with much more.

This book creates a comprehensive model of Earth and of

the entire world, studying its shape, boundaries, characteristics, and social circumstances, using reasoning and accurate facts. This research of the true shape and nature of Earth is done from all perspectives: scientific, empiric, social, cognitive, existential, and spiritual.

ABOUT THE AUTHOR

Valentin Leonard Matcas, M.Ed., is a researcher, physicist, mathematician, educator, and an author of nonfiction and fiction books, including the entire "Human" book series. Valentin Leonard Matcas wrote the "Human" book series in the following order: "The Human Needs", "The Human Addictions," "The Hierarchy of Needs," "Stay in Shape, Lead a Healthy Life," "The Human Origins," "The Human Society," "The Human Conspiracy," "The Human Mind," "The Human Reality," "Astral Planes and Your Other Realities," "Life," "The Hierarchy of Intelligences," "The Human Intelligences," "The Human Thoughts," "Mental Models and Successful Ideas," "The Human Attitudes," "The Human Stereotypes," "The Human Ideology," "Modes of Life," "The Human Development," "Patterns of Development," "The Human Lifestyle," "Heal Yourself," "The Human Civilization," "The Human Religion and Spirituality," "The Human Rights," "Higher Laws," "Natural Laws of the Universe," "Existence," "The Human Condition", "Lifelines of Causality," "The Human Behavior," "Flat Earth," "The Human Environment," "The Human Meaning," "The Human Reasoning," "The Human Interconnectivity," "The Consensual Matrix," "The Matrix of Life," and "The Human Knowledge."
Valentin Leonard Matcas writes about terrestrial and alien civilizations, about life in the universe, the way it develops and intertwines across galaxies, about powerful beings as they control and reshape the universe, and about normal living human beings from Earth caught in this beautiful, wider, outstanding interconnectivity. Valentin Leonard Matcas creates a living, warmer universe in his books, teaming with life and vibrancy, on all levels of existence. Valentin Leonard Matcas also wrote "The Storyteller" book series, including "The Storyteller," "Starship Colonial," and "Unlimited," and "The Culling" book series, including "The Culling," "The Dream of the Dead," and "The Last Man on Earth."

When he does not work on his books, Valentin Leonard Matcas enjoys researching, hiking, swimming, kayaking, skiing, snowboarding, biking, reading, listening to music, and playing strategy videogames. You may discover all his books, videos, and articles.